Fast Track

BUTTERFLY GARDENING

Fast Track

BUTTERFLY GARDENING

Rose M. Franklin

Copyright © 2012 by Rose M. Franklin

All rights reserved under International and
Pan-American Copyright Conventions.
No part of this book may be stored, reproduced, or
transmitted in any form or by any means without
the written permission of the author, except by a
reviewer who may quote brief passages in a review.

Printed in the United States of America

*I dedicate this book to
my wonderful parents,
William T. Sweeley
and
Adeline L. Sweeley,
who lovingly nurtured
their brood of nine
to adulthood and beyond.*

Table of Contents

Acknowledgments xi
Preface xii
Introduction xiv
How To Use This Book xv

Part I: My Journey to Butterfly Gardening 3
A Childhood Fascination 3
The Fascination Gets Rekindled 3
The Ever-Evolving Butterfly Garden 5

Part II: Getting To Know Butterflies 9
Butterfly Anatomy 101 9
The Metamorphosis of a Butterfly 11
The Metamorphosis of a Monarch Butterfly 14
The Metamorphosis of a Baltimore Checkerspot Butterfly 15

Part III: Planning the Butterfly Garden 18
Location and Design Considerations 18
Butterfly Nectar Plants 19
Caterpillar Host Plants 20
A Table Of Host Plants 21
Narrowing the Host Plant Choices 24
On Behalf of All Butterflies 25
Reaping The Rewards Of Host Plant Incorporation 25

Part IV: The Best-of-the-Best Butterfly Attracting Plants 28
Why The Disagreement? 28
How I Choose the Best-Of-The-Best 29
Butterfly Bush 30
Purple Coneflower 31
Garden Phlox 'Jeana' 32
Tropical Milkweed 33

Swamp Milkweed 34
Common Milkweed 35
Butterfly Weed..36
Meadow Blazing Star 37
Coreopsis 'Early Sunrise' 38
Zinnia 39
Brazilian Verbena 40
Mexican Sunflower 40
Scabiosa 'Butterfly Blue' 41
Joe-Pye Weed..41
Cosmos 42
Verbena 'Homestead Purple' 42
Stonecrop 'Autumn Joy' 43
Lilac 43
Artemisia 'Silver Brocade' 44
Rue (also known as Herb-of-Grace)..................................44

Part V: The Butterflies You Might See In Your Garden 48
The Dances of Butterflies 48
The Romantic Dance of Two Giant Swallowtails 48
Choosing The Featured Butterflies....................................49
Giant Swallowtail...51
Tiger Swallowtail 52
Spicebush Swallowtail 53
Black Swallowtail 54
Monarch 55
Red-Spotted Purple 56
White Admiral 57
Mourning Cloak 58
Viceroy...59
Aphrodite Fritillary 60
Variegated Fritillary 61
Painted Lady 62
Red Admiral...63
Hackberry Emperor 64
Clouded Sulphur 65
Question Mark 66

Buckeye 67
Milbert's Tortoiseshell 68
Baltimore Checkerspot 69
Meadow Fritillary 70
Cabbage White 71
Gray Hairstreak 72
Pearl Crescent..73
Eastern Tailed Blue 74

Part VI: Sharing The Sources 78
Books 78
Field Guides 78
Websites 79
An Invitation to Explore My Website 81

Glossary of Butterfly Terminology 84

Acknowledgments

When I graduated from high school in 1969, I had three aspirations: to get married, to have children, and to author a book. By 2010, forty-one years later, I had twice been a bride, had two grown sons, but still had not put down on paper anything that even remotely resembled a book. It was time to end the procrastination.

In my twenties and thirties, I thought my book might be a love-story paperback, but I outgrew that idea in my forties. For the next ten years or so, I contemplated the notion of writing a book about gardening with perennials, a topic I now knew something about. But I never felt compelled to write at length on the subject of perennials.

During my forties and fifties, I was infatuated with butterfly gardening, and butterfly photography was my favorite hobby. I had written numerous articles on butterfly gardening and had enjoyed doing that.

At fifty-nine, a few days after Christmas, I announced to my husband, mother, and sister that I was going to write a book on butterfly gardening. My book would be a replica of the one I would have liked to have found in my early days of butterfly gardening.

During the winter of 2010-2011, I wrote a minimum of ten hours a day. Late at night I would type, proofread, and then write some more. Often I would get up in the middle of the night to jot down fragments of ideas that had aroused my mind and awakened me from sleep. Having little time for exercise, television, or even conversing with my husband, I came to understand why authors sometimes live as hermits.

While I had already taken lots of photographs of butterflies and plants over the past twenty years, I knew by spring that I would need more. My manuscript yearned for images I did not have. During the summer of 2011, I took a few hundred more photos. In mid November though, after the butterflies had all disappeared for the season, I realized that I was still missing some photos I had hoped to incorporate into the book.

At that point, I reached out to friends—and to strangers—for the photos I needed. Jim Nero, Edith Smith, Tom Pawlesh, Paul Chesterfield, Michael Keniston, and Tatia Veltkamp all came forward with beautiful images I was permitted to publish. In Part VI of the book, I give a brief description of who each of these contributors are. Here I will simply say "thank you" to each of them. My son, Rob, sketched a drawing of a Saddleback caterpillar that you will see in Part V of the book. To him too, I am grateful for his time and effort.

From my first weeks of writing until the finish in April, 2012, I had friends and relatives doing the proofreading. Joe Kunst, my neighbor and close friend, and Bob Snetsinger, my friend and mentor in entomological study, both offered valuable advice in the organization and layout of the book, along with preliminary proofreading.

My mom, Adeline Sweeley; two daughters-in-law, Jodie LeFevre-Franklin and Joy Bogel; friends, John and Catherine Smith, Jim Searfoss, and Judith Fordham; and husband, Andrew Smith, all read and reread the manuscript looking for typographical errors. Paul Rentschler, a computer wizard, offered technical expertise several times when I desperately needed it. Alex and Jason of Wolfpack Design converted my PageMaker files into PDFs so that the pages of my book could be printed

To all these people, I offer my sincere thanks. I very much appreciate the time each of them dedicated so that my teenage aspiration could finally evolve to become reality.

Preface

In publishing this book I hope to inspire others to get involved in gardening for butterflies. Many butterfly species are fighting for survival, and butterfly gardeners could be instrumental in their revival. As of April, 2012, the U.S. Fish & Wildlife Service listed 62 insect species on the Endangered or Threatened Species List. Of those, almost half are butterflies.

While there are no butterfly census reports to refer to, the consensus is that the butterfly population in the U.S. has declined by as much as 40% in the past 40 years and that, without intervention, the number of butterflies will likely continue to dwindle. What has caused this sharp decline in the number of butterflies? Most entomologists claim the leading causes are likely (1) the use of insecticides, and (2) the destruction of natural habitat. Some cite the effects of global warming as a contributing factor.

Since the introduction of chemical insecticides after World War II, homeowners have waged a massive attack on insects. In protecting our prized flowers, shrubs, and trees from aphids, mites, and Japanese Beetles though, we have poisoned butterflies too. Unable to distinguish between an aphid and a butterfly, most insecticides simply kill them both.

Since the 1970s, vast areas of forest have been aerial sprayed with insecticides (first DDT, then later Bt) to control the Gypsy Moth larvae. These larvae are highly destructive and threaten to defoliate and kill our forest trees, especially the oaks and elms. But through efforts to eradicate the Gypsy Moth, many woodland butterfly species have fallen victim to the assault. Butterflies were not the intended targets of the spraying but they have certainly suffered the consequences, being killed off by the thousands.

As if insecticides alone have not been enough of an attack on the butterfly population, we have added to their demise through the destruction of natural habitat. Wildflower meadows that once were utilized by butterflies for nectaring, mating, and egg-laying are being transformed into housing developments, golf courses, and shopping malls. Forests are being destroyed by heavy equipment to construct new resorts, apartment complexes, highways, and bridges. We dig up and clear out indigenous butterfly attracting plants and replace them with exotic flowers, shrubs, and trees that are of no benefit to butterflies. In many locations, butterflies have found survival and reproduction to be difficult at best, impossible at worst.

Once the wildflower meadows are converted to lawns and golf courses, it often becomes the property owners' aim to rid their turf of weeds. But in spraying lawns with herbicides to kill the broad-leaved plants, we are wiping out some of the plants that butterflies need for survival. Among these are Plantain, which is utilized by several butterfly species as a food source, and Sweet Violets, which are of vital importance in the life cycle of the genus of butterflies know as Fritillaries.

We cannot allow the butterfly population to continue in a downward spiral. Butterflies, like every creature on earth, have important roles. They are important to the food chain. Butterfly eggs, larvae, and pupae are utilized as food by other insects, birds, reptiles, amphibians, and rodents. For every one hundred butterfly eggs that are laid, only two will likely reach the stage of adulthood. The other 98% will be consumed by predators in their own quest to stay alive. But this is the way nature intended it to be, and so long as 2% ultimately survive to replace their parents and reproduce, the butterfly population remains essentially the same. When a portion of this 2% is wiped out, say by insecticides, the destruction of natural habitat, or the effects of global warming, the butterfly population declines. Unfortunately, one, two, or possibly all three of these factors seem to have taken their toll in recent years.

Butterflies assist other insects in the pollination of flowers. While bees and wasps are the main pollinators, butterflies also transfer pollen from one flower's stamen to another flower's pistol, thus allowing fruit and seed to mature.

If lots of butterflies are present in a given area, it usually indicates that there are a lot of other insects in the vicinity too. Where insects are plentiful, the environment as a whole is typically healthy. A lack of insects generally indicates that the environment is not as healthy as it might, and probably should, be.

For us though, the most important reason we may have for helping butterflies in their quest to survive is simply so we will always have them. They adorn our gardens with mystical beauty and whimsical flight. They enchant us, delight us, mesmerize us, and amaze us. Who wants to imagine a world without butterflies?

Introduction

I am not an entomologist; nor do I consider myself an expert on butterflies. I am able to identify about fifty butterfly species and for most of those, I cannot easily distinguish a male from a female. But I have no desire to become an expert on butterflies. My aspiration lies only in wanting to increase the number of butterflies that reside in my backyard, both the number of butterfly species and the number of individuals within a species.

My first butterfly garden was planted in 1993, and since then, I have improved upon it dramatically. Every winter I plan for the changes that will be made the following spring. Each spring the gardens are modified with the expectation that they will perform better than before.

During the summer, plants are rated and ranked in their ability to attract butterflies. If they rank high, they remain in the garden. When one ranks low, it is removed, and then replaced by another plant.

For nineteen years I have followed this pattern of planting, ranking, and then replanting. But my efforts have proven to be worth the investment. Now, on any warm summer day, my yard is laden with butterflies. It's commonplace to see thirty or forty at any given time. Monarchs, Swallowtails, Red-Spotted Purples, Fritillaries, Sulphurs, Buckeyes, American Ladies, and more adorn our gardens with their beauty, charisma, and charm.

I have written this book so others can skip years of trial and tribulation in searching for the best-of-the-best butterfly attracting plants. My goal is to put beginning butterfly gardeners on the fast track to more advanced butterfly gardening.

By reading this book and following some of my suggestions, you too should have butterflies visiting your garden. Even in your first year of butterfly gardening, you should notice that butterflies are more abundant than ever before, and as you keep adding butterfly attracting plants to your property, the number will only increase.

May your adventure in butterfly gardening be a very rewarding experience!

Rose M. Franklin

How To Use This Book

Whether you are a novice or a semi-pro at butterfly gardening, you will likely find something of interest within the pages of this book. The book is divided into six sections.

In Part I, "My Path to Butterfly Gardening", I explain how my childhood fascination of watching butterflies ultimately grew to become an adult passion for helping butterflies to survive and multiply in a world that has grown to be somewhat hostile toward them.

Part II, "Getting To Know Butterflies", looks at butterfly anatomy, butterfly behavior, and the butterfly life cycle. Once you understand the various aspects of a butterfly's life you will be better prepared to create a haven in which they will flourish.

In Part III, "Planning A Garden For Butterflies", you'll learn where to plant, and how to design, a garden that will lure butterflies. You will also be introduced to the concept of caterpillar host plants and learn why and how you might incorporate some of them into your landscape.

Part IV, "The Best-Of-The-Best Butterfly Attracting Plants", illustrates and describes the plants which I highly recommend for incorporation into your butterfly garden. By designing a garden that includes a number of these plants, you will be on the fast track to successful butterfly gardening.

Part V, "The Butterflies That Might Visit Your Butterfly Garden", illustrates and describes some of the butterflies that are commonly seen in butterfly gardens. For each butterfly species illustrated, I will explain where in the U.S. you are most likely to see it, what months you are most likely see it, what flowers (and/or fruits) it often feeds on, what some of its host plants are, and in what stage of life it over-winters. On some pages, where space permitted, I inserted blocks of information that, I hope, you find important and/or interesting.

In Part VI, "Sharing the Sources", I list some of the books, field guides, and websites I have enjoyed in my nineteen years of butterfly gardening. You too might want to explore some of these. Part VI concludes with information on how to contact me.

If you find typographical errors in the book, please let me know. If you have a suggestion on how to make the book better, I'd like to hear about that too. Who knows. Maybe in ten years I'll publish a revised edition of the book to incorporate some of the suggestions made by the readers of this edition.

Part I
My Journey To Butterfly Gardening

On this farm, located near the small town of Spring Mills, Pennsylvania, I grew up. The oldest of nine children, I loved animals, enjoyed the outdoors, and was fascinated by the butterflies which appeared on the farm every summer. As an adult, my fascination would be rekindled and I would develop a passion for studying and photographing butterflies. That passion would eventually lead to the writing of this book.

Part I: My Journey to Butterfly Gardening

A Childhood Fascination

Around the age of twelve, I developed a fascination for butterflies. My family lived on a 150 acre dairy farm in central Pennsylvania and it was there that butterflies first caught my attention. The long dirt lane that led from the macadam road to our house and barn was dotted with puddles following every summer rain. Soon after the sun appeared from behind the clouds though, the muddy edges of the puddles were speckled with butterflies. Believing the butterflies had congregated around the puddles because they were thirsty, I did not disturb them. Instead, quietly, I stood near by and watched them come and go. Some of the butterflies were tiny with wings of blue, some were medium sized with wings of yellow and gray, others were large, decorated in vivid black and yellow stripes. Different sizes, different colors, different shapes; but every butterfly was an amazing creature that captivated my attention.

Bordering our huge vegetable garden (it took a huge garden to feed our family, which consisted of my parents and their nine children) were long rows of flowers: Gladiolas, Zinnias, Marigolds, and Sweet Peas. Fluttering from Zinnia to Zinnia on warm summer days were butterflies. They didn't congregate on the Gladiolas, but they sure did flock to the Zinnias. Looking out over the vegetable garden into the bordering Alfalfa field, scores of medium-sized white and yellow butterflies could be seen skipping and dancing among the pale lavender blossoms.

In the cow pasture, where Thistle and Milkweed grew among the grasses that were eaten by the cattle, butterflies of various size and color fluttered and sailed from flower to flower in search of nectar. There in the pasture, butterflies seemed equally attracted to both the Milkweed and Thistle blooms. Butterflies even landed on the cow patties that speckled the pasture's ground and actually appeared to be feeding there. Back then, I couldn't understand why a butterfly would dine on cow poop instead of sweet flower nectar when it always had the choice.

There on the farm I was fascinated and amazed by butterflies. But then I grew up, got married, and moved away from the family homestead in 1969. For the next twenty years I rarely saw butterflies around the homes where I lived. Never questioning their absence, I simply assumed that butterflies live on farms.

From my mother, I acquired a love for flowers, so as an adult my home was always adorned with common blooming plants. Rose bushes, Geraniums, Celosia, Petunias, and Marigolds edged the border of our yard during my early years of marriage. Later I acquired an interest in perennials and added Astilbe, Hosta, Shasta Daisy, Baby's Breath, Veronica, and others to the landscape. While I had beautiful gardens, I didn't have butterflies. Had I known then what I know now, I would have planted a palate of irresistible nectar flowers that would have enticed the butterflies to come.

The Fascination Gets Rekindled

Through my twenties and thirties, I worked as a waitress, a secretary, and a floral designer, managing my own flower shop for twelve years. By the early 1980s, floral industry leaders were predicting that grocery stores would soon be incorporating full-service floral departments and that, as a result, flower shops would likely see a sharp decline in business.

In 1986, then recently divorced, with two sons in high school, and no computer skills, I heeded the warning and enrolled as a student at Penn State University to advance my education so I could obtain work in another field if necessary. During my first three years of college I kept the flower shop open but rearranged the hours of operation to accommodate my classes.

Just prior to the start of my senior year of college, devastation struck. I lost my home to foreclosure. And not only did I lose my home but also my job because the flower shop had occupied the front portion of the house. With no home, no job, and no saving account, my sons and I moved in with my parents.

It was early September, and I was back on the farm. Dairy cows still grazed in the pasture and the lane was still pebbles and dirt. I guess the butterflies were still there too, but I didn't see them. I was sad, bitter, depressed, and broken.

I found a part time job as a nurses' aide in a nearby mental hospital and six months later, in May of 1991, I graduated from Penn State. With a B.S. in Human Development and Family Studies, my position at the hospital was immediately upgraded to full-time.

Life was looking (and feeling) brighter. I enjoyed my work, was receiving weekly paychecks (which regularly included pay for overtime), and I had formed close bonds with a few coworkers. Confident all was going well, I purchased a used mobile home and moved it onto a lot that bordered my parents' property. A year later, I and thirty other employees were permanently laid off at work.

Over the next few months, I applied for work at scores of places but was not successful in landing a job. Desperate for an income, I decided to grow perennial plants on my property and then haul them off to flea markets to sell.

And so it was in the spring of 1992 that I invested a few hundred dollars to purchase flower seed, potting soil, and pots that were to yield a huge profit when I sold the finished plants at market.

Among the many packets of seed I purchased were a few labeled 'Bloodflower'. I had never heard of this flower before but the seed packets proclaimed the plants to be tender perennials that would produce clusters of orange and yellow star-shaped flowers which would attract butterflies.

I planted the Bloodflower seeds in trays. They germinated in about ten days, quickly outgrew the seedling trays, and were transplanted into 4" pots. By early July, the plants were bushy, gorgeously green, and beginning to produce buds. These beauties would soon be going to market!

A week later I noticed tiny holes in the leaves of the Bloodflower plants and then, a week after that, dozens of inch-long, yellow, black, and white striped "worms". Worried the worms were going to completely defoliate my beautiful plants, I plucked them from the leaves, threw them on the ground, and stomped on them. For the remainder of the summer, I continued to pick worms from the plants because, just like weeds, they kept appearing. By mid-September, I had rid my plants of at least fifty ugly, destructive worms.

I couldn't understand why these brightly-colored, poisonous-looking creatures had been abundant on the Bloodflowers but were not on any of the plants that were growing in pots right next to them. Wanting explanation, I made a visit to Pattee Library at Penn State University that winter. After a few hours of paging through books on gardening, I finally found a picture of the "worms" I had killed. Astonished and ashamed, I realized then that I had destroyed over fifty caterpillars which would have matured to become majestic Monarch butterflies.

Sitting at a library table that afternoon, I learned that the reason the Monarch caterpillars had been on the Bloodflower foliage was that this plant belonged to the Milkweed family, and that Milkweed is the host plant for Monarch caterpillars. I left Pattee Library that day with an armload of books on butterflies and butterfly gardening. For the next several months, I read

A Monarch caterpillar on Bloodflower (also known as Tropical Milkweed and/or Mexican Milkweed).

as much as I could on the subject of gardening for butterflies. I made lists of butterfly-attracting plants and learned the names of some of the butterfly species that might visit a butterfly garden in central Pennsylvania.

To my surprise, I learned that butterflies do not require easy access to mud puddles, cow poop, Alfalfa, Milkweed, and Thistle blossoms. Even residing in an urban community, a butterfly gardener could realistically expect to attract at least four or five species of butterflies; and a person living in a rural setting might attract many more. It wasn't because I had left the farm that I hadn't seen many butterflies in the past twenty years. It was simply that I hadn't planted the flowers that butterflies seek.

That same winter, I ran across an article that had appeared in the July/August issue of *Organic Gardening* entitled, "Grow Your Own Butterflies". The article was about a man named Rick Mikula who lived in northeastern Pennsylvania and reared butterflies in his backyard, and even in his house! During his interview with one of the magazine's writers, Mr. Mikula stated that Monarchs are among the easiest of butterflies to rear. "Really?", I whispered to myself. "Wow!" I was suddenly inspired to raise butterflies too. Feeling guilty and sad over having killed several dozen Monarch caterpillars, I felt obligated to hand-rear enough Monarchs to replace what I had robbed from nature the summer before.

My childhood interest in butterflies had been rekindled. The seeds were planted for what would become a long, rewarding adventure in butterfly gardening, butterfly rearing, and butterfly photography.

In the nineteen years that followed, I planted many butterfly gardens, tested and rated hundreds of plant species for their attractiveness to butterflies, reared thousands of Monarchs (and hundreds of Swallowtails, Ladies, and Baltimores too), and captured scores of butterflies on film (more recently, on SD cards). My tiny perennial plant nursery eventually evolved to become an operation large enough to keep myself and several others busy all summer long.

The Ever-Evolving Butterfly Garden

My first butterfly garden was planted in 1993. It included many of the plants that were highly recommended in the books and articles I had read the previous winter. Gloriosa Daisy, Yarrow, Gaillardia, Kansas Gayfeather, Sedum, Garden Phlox, Butterfly Weed, Butterfly Bush (all perennials), Zinnia, Marigolds, Bloodflower, Cosmos, and Lantana (all annuals) all made their appearance in my first butterfly garden. The summer ended with me being absolutely amazed by the number of butterflies that visited the garden for nectar. So too was I astonished by the number of Monarch butterflies that grew up on the Bloodflower (also known as Tropical Milkweed and Mexican Milkweed) that had been planted in the garden.

The following year I added some Purple Coneflowers, Coreopsis, Swamp Milkweed, and Joe-Pye Weed. That summer butterflies flocked to the four new additions but completely ignored some of the plants they had utilized as nectar sources the year before. I theorized then that when butterflies don't have their favorite nectar sources available to them, they simply settle for whatever is available. When their favorites are handy, though, they congregate at those and reduce visitation to the second-rate nectar sources. When humans have a choice between a tender, tasty steak or a dry, burnt hamburger, they'll usually take the steak. When steak is not available, however, and the person is very hungry, he or she might be grateful for the burnt hamburger.

In the years that followed, I added more flower species to the garden every year. Then I watched anxiously to see which of those plants the butterflies flocked to. Some years I even created crude charts to track each plant's attraction to butterflies.

Once I acquired an interest (which was actually more like an obsession) in gardening for butterflies, I began choosing for my nursery those plants that were proclaimed by others to attract butterflies. I occasionally asked my wholesalers to take note of what plants attracted butterflies in their trial gardens. When I received a suggestion from someone, I ordered a flat of that plant species so I could test it in one of my gardens. The plants that ranked high in attracting butterflies were given a permanent spot in the garden while those that ranked low were never planted again.

By the time the summer of 1999 came to a close, my butterfly gardens were doing a fantastic job of attracting butterflies. On the other hand, though, my perennial nursery was still not producing much of an income. Some weeks I did reasonably well at flea markets, others I barely made enough money to pay for the fuel and lot rent.

It seemed time to look for a real job. But I enjoyed growing plants, and I had so much knowledge to share on the subject of gardening for butterflies. I had tested plants in trial gardens, ranked their ability to attract butterflies, and knew exactly how to put others on the fast track to successful butterfly gardening. I just hadn't found a way to reach the people that were seriously interested in creating butterfly habitats.

That winter I created and launched a website, www.ButterflyBushes.com. On the website, I provided lots of information on butterfly gardening, and also offered many of the plants I had found to be excellent butterfly-attracting plants. I included an order form that customers could print, fill out, and mail to me with a check. Customers could not, however, use credit cards for payment. Orders began to trickle in.

In following winters I optimized the website to boost my ranking with search engines and to increase traffic to the site. I asked related gardening websites to provide a link from their site to mine. I added a shopping cart so that orders could be placed electronically and payment could be made using a credit card. Business dramatically increased with every passing year.

Since 2000, I have continued to test different plant species in my trial gardens. Until I am too old and feeble to garden, my butterfly gardens will likely evolve and transform with every passing summer. And so too will the website change to reflect the new discoveries I make over time.

Prior to launching the website, I felt for years as though I were inside a hard shell which I could not break out of. My little perennial business had grown and developed to become a nursery that specialized in offering the best-of-the-best butterfly-attracting plants. It yearned to be discovered. I somehow had to crack the shell that was encasing me. In launching the website, I was able to introduce to an interested audience the nursery I had created and nurtured in a location where few people knew it existed.

Today my website business is doing well. I am healthy, happily married, proud of my two sons and the families they blessed me with, and my yard is alive with butterflies. I couldn't ask for more.

Part II
Getting To Know
Butterflies

8   Fast Track Butterfly Gardening

Excerpts from the Life of a Monarch

1. Monarch eggs on a Milkweed emerging in spring.
2. Monarch caterpillars (larvae).
3. Monarch caterpillar shedding its skin.
4. Monarch caterpillar prepared to pupate.
5. Monarch pupa (chrysalis).
6. Monarch pupa just prior to the butterfly's emergence.
7. Monarch emerging from pupa (eclosure).
8. A pair of Monarchs mating.
9. Monarch feeding on nectar.

Part II: Getting To Know Butterflies

Butterfly Anatomy 101

Butterflies are insects. Like all insects, each butterfly has three pair of legs and three main body parts: a head, a thorax, and an abdomen. An insect has no bones but instead, an exoskeleton, a hard covering or skin on the outside of its body.

A Giant Swallowtail, closeup

Butterflies belong to the order of insects known as **Lepidoptera**, along with moths. Lepidoptera means "scaly wings". Butterflies are divided into two superfamilies: the true butterflies and the skippers. True butterflies can generally be distinguished from skippers by being more colorful and having narrower bodies and longer antennae. (See page 68.)

A butterfly's head is composed of two huge eyes, two antennae, and a proboscis. Its large eyes enable it to see in every direction without turning its head. The butterfly's antennae are equipped with chemical receptors that serve the function of smelling. They are also used for balance when the butterfly is in flight. At the end of each antenna is a swollen knob. It is this knob-like antenna tip that usually serves to distinguish a butterfly from a moth. A moth's antennae are most often feather-like or plain. The proboscis is

The feather-like antennae identify this Lepidoptera as a moth.

a straw-like mouthpart which is used for sucking nectar from flowers and water from puddles. Unable to chew solid foods, a butterfly's diet is exclusively liquid.

A butterfly's thorax is composed of three body segments. Each of the three thoracic segments bears a pair of jointed legs which have taste receptors on the bottoms of them. The thorax also bears the wings. Each of the two pair of wings is comprised of a forewing (the wing closest to the butterfly's head) and a hindwing (the wing closest to the butterfly's abdomen). The wings are paper-thin and covered with thousands of tiny fish-like scales which can only be seen under a microscope. The scales slightly overlap each other like shingles on a roof. Some male butterflies have special scales which emit an enticing scent during courtship.

In some butterfly species, the front pair of legs is shorter than the other two pair of legs. Especially true of the males in this large family of butterflies, their front legs are too short to even be used for walking. They are however, equipped with the receptors that serve an important role in tasting. Among the species that fall into this large group of shortened-front-legged butterflies is the well known Monarch.

A butterfly's abdomen is composed of ten body segments and contains the reproductive organs. Digestive, circulatory, and excretory functions also occur in the abdomen. Since only liquids are consumed by butterflies, only liquids are excreted. The tip of a female's abdomen is generally rounded while the male's is equipped with a set of "claspers". When butterflies mate, the male's claspers will open and then clamp down on the female's abdomen. Mating pairs are easy to spot as they will be attached at their abdomens and facing opposite directions.

Monarch abdomens: female on left, male on right

Mating Monarchs

Like other insects, butterflies have no lungs. They breathe through tiny holes located in their thorax and abdomen. The holes are known as **spiracles**.

Butterflies are cold-blooded insects and are not able to fly when the air temperature is too low. Unable to warm their flight muscles on brisk, cloudy days, they are physically unable to take wing. This is why you do not see butterflies flying about when the air is cool. Technically, a butterfly doesn't have blood but instead a blood-like substance called hemolymph. This blood-like substance is not red but rather a translucent yellowish color.

Being cold-blooded creatures that are unable to generate their own body heat, butterflies often bask in the sun to warm their bodies in preparation for flight. Sometimes they sit on vegetation to bask but often they will sit on a rock or cling to the side of a building, orienting their bodies toward the sun.

It may not be just by coincidence that most butterflies have dark colored bodies and wing bases. Since dark colors absorb more heat from the sun than light colors do, butterflies may have evolved over time to have bodies that are dark in color.

Some butterflies tend to gather around puddles or along the edges of streams and ponds. This common behavior is known as **puddling** and scientists have discovered that butterflies frequent these locations to extract salts and other nutrients from the moist soil. It tends to be male butterflies that congregate at the edges of puddles, streams, and ponds, and it is believed that they need the extracted nutrients for reproductive purposes. The nutrients might be needed by the male, or they may be passed on to the female during mating. Among the butterflies that commonly engage in puddling are Swallowtails (large butterflies), Blues (tiny butterflies), and Sulphurs (medium-sized butterflies).

In some butterfly species the males are larger than the females. In others, the females are larger than the males. For many species, both sexes are the same size, but somewhere on their wing is a tiny, subtle marking that identifies them as male or female.

Butterflies are only active during the day. During the night they roost, sometimes high above the ground, often on the undersides of leaves. Only rarely will you spot a butterfly at rest though, as each tends to be well camouflaged wherever it roosts.

Some butterflies have wings that are brightly colored on top but dull on the undersides. These butterflies generally rest with closed wings on tree bark where their wings almost perfectly blend into the bark, thus protecting them from predators.

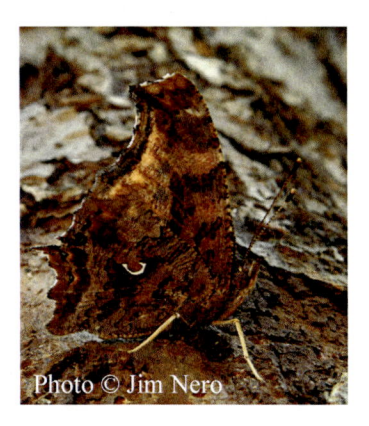

With its wings closed, this Comma butterfly blends into the tree bark it is resting on.

Watching butterflies in a meadow or garden, you might think they leisurely fly about all day long. Actually they do not. Because predators lurk everywhere, a butterfly stays hidden except when necessity calls it into the open. When a butterfly is not in hiding, it is feeding, looking for a potential mate, or, if the butterfly is a female, laying eggs.

Some butterflies live for only a week or two as an adult so reproduction is of high importance to ensure the survival of the species. Some species of butterflies produce just one generation of offspring per year, whereas others produce two, three, or more. Entomologists don't speak of butterfly generations though. They refer to butterfly "broods". A **brood** includes all of the butterflies that are borne from the same female. Think of the brood as all of the sisters and brothers in a butterfly family.

While butterflies actually see a wider spectrum of colors than humans see, they cannot see detail from a distance. This becomes evident when you watch a male butterfly that is searching for a mate. If the male is, for instance, a Monarch, he will dart at every orange colored butterfly he sees. Not until he gets up close can he distinguish between a Monarch and a Great Spangled Fritillary, both of which are predominately orange.

Most butterflies feed on flower nectar. A few though, rarely or never feed on nectar. These butterflies gather nutrients from rotting fruit, tree sap, mammal manure, or decaying animal carcasses.

Some butterflies have brightly colored spots on the tips of their wings. These spots likely serve to protect the butterfly's vital body parts in vicious bird attacks. If a hungry bird aims for the bright spot on the butterfly's wing, its beak will miss the butterfly's head, thorax, and abdomen. And since most butterflies are able to fly with only half a wing, they will still be able to escape. If you closely observe butterflies, you will notice that some of them have "V"-shaped notches cut from the outer edges of their wings. Most often, these butterflies were the victims of bird attacks.

There are four stages of development in a butterfly's life, and every stage is distinctively different from the one which preceded it. Every butterfly begins life as an egg, which hatches to reveal a caterpillar (the larval stage), which then becomes encased inside a chrysalis (the pupal stage), which eventually cracks open to display an adult butterfly. The whole process of going from egg to caterpillar to chrysalis to adult is known as metamorphosis.

The Metamorphosis of a Butterfly

The metamorphosis of a butterfly can take from three weeks to over a year depending upon the butterfly species. A Monarch butterfly generally goes from an egg to an adult in about a month while it takes a Baltimore Checkerspot butterfly ten to eleven months to complete its metamorphosis.

Female butterflies lay their eggs on or near a **host plant**, a plant which will provide food for her caterpillars. Host plants will be covered in great detail later in this book (see page 19). Butterfly eggs are different in size, shape, and color depending upon the butterfly species. Some are only the size of the periods at the end of the sentences in this book while others are 1/8" in diameter. They may be round or oval; white, yellow, green, pink, or blue. Many are one color when they are laid but then change color prior to hatching. Some butterfly species lay their eggs singly while others lay their eggs in clusters of seventy-five or more. A single female can lay 300 eggs or more during the short course of her adulthood. Once the eggs are laid, butterflies take no responsibility in the rearing of their offspring.

Butterfly eggs usually, but certainly not always, hatch in about a week. The tiny caterpillar (larva) chews its way out of the egg, generally eats its eggshell, and then begins to nibble on the host plant. During the larval stage which, depending upon the butterfly species, may last less than two weeks or might last many months, the caterpillar molts (sheds its skin) four times. The intervals between molts are known as **instars**. Caterpillars are miniature eating machines and some can actually double in size in a 24 hour period.

Caterpillars come in endless color combinations. Some have bright yellow, orange, or blue on their bodies while others are dull brown, pale green, or black and white. Some are decorated with brightly colored eye spots while others are camouflaged to look like bird droppings. Some are smooth while others are hairy. Some have knobs, bumps, or bristles on their bodies. Others have fleshy filament-like projections near their head or tail. A few have a horn-like projection protruding from their abdomen.

Just like an adult butterfly, each caterpillar has a head, a thorax, and an abdomen. On the head are its antennae, its eyes, and its mouth. Caterpillars have very poor eyesight, being able to distinguish little more than day from night. But they have an excellent sense of smell (with olfactory receptors on the tips of their antennae) and taste (with receptors in their mouth and also on the bottom of their legs). Some caterpillars have antennae which are so small you can't even see them. A Monarch caterpillar appears to have two pair of antennae, one pair near its head and another pair near its tail. Technically, the rear fleshy tentacles are not antennae, but they are believed to function as sense organs.

Just under its head, a caterpillar has an apparatus known as a **spinneret**. Inside the spinneret are glands which secrete a liquid that, when exposed to air, forms silk-like strands. These silk strands are utilized by caterpillars in various ways. They sometimes secure the caterpillar to the surface it is walking on. They can also be used to suspend the caterpillar in midair if it must escape a predator. Some caterpillar species use the silk strands to tie the edges of leaves together so they will be hidden from predators inside the folded foliage. In some species, the caterpillars work together to create a dense, web-like structure to surround themselves as they feed communally on plant foliage.

The thorax is comprised of three segments, each having a pair of jointed legs. These are not however, the same three pair of legs that the butterfly will possess. The caterpillar's legs, and many other tissues too, will be broken down and digested in the next stage of development.

Four caterpillars:
Monarch, top left;
Spicebush Swallowtail, top right;
Giant Swallowtail, bottom left;
Baltimore Checkerspot, bottom right

The abdomen is composed of ten body segments and includes another five pair of legs that are referred to as ***prolegs***. The prolegs will not appear on the adult butterfly but are necessary in the larval stage to aid the caterpillar in crawling from leaf to leaf, or plant to plant, in search of food.

When the caterpillar is fully grown, it stops eating, often crawls off the plant it had been feeding on, and seeks a safe place to pupate. The spot it chooses for pupating may be just a few inches, or more than twenty feet, from where it last feasted. Just before many butterfly species pupate, the caterpillar utilizes its spinneret to produce a silk-like mat. Once the mat is laid, the caterpillar crawls forward, attaches its ***cremaster*** (a hook-like apparatus located on the end of the caterpillar's abdomen) to the mat, and then allows its body to drop downward. There the caterpillar hangs upside down in a "J" shape, usually for several hours. Then suddenly its skin splits open and is shed from its entire body. Under the caterpillar's shed skin is a soft shell called a ***chrysalis***. The chrysalis hardens in a few hours to become a hard protective casing.

As is the case with butterfly eggs and caterpillars, chrysalises are different sizes, shapes, and colors depending upon the butterfly species. Some are smooth while others have jagged looking edges. Some are shiny green while others are dull gray or brown.

Inside the chrysalis (the pupal stage of development), miraculous changes take place. The mouth is transformed from being the cutting and chewing devise that was necessary for the caterpillar to eat plant foliage to being an apparatus that can be used by the adult butterfly to probe into flowers and suck up nectar. This newly formed apparatus, the ***proboscis***, is tubular and functions as a retractable drinking straw, allowing the butterfly to feed only on liquids. When not in use, the proboscis will be coiled up and out of the butterfly's way. Wings grow on its thorax and the prolegs disappear from the abdomen. Reproductive organs, which were absent in the larval stage, appear. The creepy, crawling creature evolves to become one of the most beautiful flying insects on earth. I often tell kids that the pupal stage in a butterfly's life is where the ugly duckling becomes a beautiful swan.

When the transformation from caterpillar to butterfly is complete, the chrysalis cracks open and a stubby, wet, crumpled butterfly tumbles out. As the butterfly emerges from its chrysalis, it is said to be ***eclosing***. Clinging tightly to its chrysalis while hemolymph is pumped through its body and wings to expand them, the butterfly will be unable to fly for an hour or more. Once the wings are fully expanded and dry, with its legs still clasping to the chrysalis, the butterfly will open and close its wings several times to exercise its flight muscles. Then suddenly off it will go on its journey to find nectar and soon, a mate.

Some butterfly species overwinter as adults, others overwinter as caterpillars, some overwinter as pupae, and a very limited number as eggs. Most of the butterflies that overwinter as adults spend the winter months in a hibernation-like state, with their hemolymph acting as an antifreeze-like substance. On warm spring days though, these butterflies sometimes temporarily come out of their dormant state in search of nectar. They may be spotted on Lilac, Dianthus, or any early blooming flower which suits the butterfly's taste. Some of the woodland butterflies seek out tree sap that may be oozing from broken branches of maple or birch trees.

Monarch butterflies are not able to withstand freezing temperatures. They overwinter as adults but escape the freezing temperatures by migrating to Mexico. There, about 80 miles southwest of Mexico City, in the Oyamel fir forests, they find refuge from frigid air. Not all Monarchs migrate to Mexico however. Some are year around residents in Florida and California.

Now we will look at the life cycles of two different butterflies: the Monarch and the Baltimore Checkerspot. Monarch butterflies complete metamorphosis in about a month whereas Baltimore Checkerspots require a period of 10 to 11 months to complete their life cycle.

The Metamorphosis of a Monarch Butterfly

Monarch females lay their eggs on Milkweed, the host plant for Monarch caterpillars. The tiny white eggs are laid singly and generally on the undersides of leaves. Each egg is attached to the leaf by an adhesive fluid that is applied to the egg as it is being laid. Five to seven days after the eggs are deposited, they will hatch.

Immediately after hatching, the caterpillar is so small it can barely be seen. It grows fast though, feeding on nothing but Milkweed. A Monarch caterpillar can eat enough Milkweed leaves in one day to equal its own body weight. Ten to fourteen days after hatching, the catepillar is full grown (about 2-1/4" long) and ready to pupate.

During its larval stage, a Monarch caterpillar will molt (shed its skin) four times. Often they will leave the host plant for molting. When molting is complete, the caterpillar will usually eat its shed skin and then return to feeding on Milkweed.

When it is ready to pupate, the caterpillar generally leaves its host plant. It crawls (sometimes 10 to 20 feet away from the Milkweed), lays down a silk-like mat, attaches its cremaster to the mat, then allows its body to drop and hang upside down in a "J" shape. About 24 hours later, the skin is shed from the caterpillar and under it, a soft jade green shell is revealed. The shell (its chrysalis) hardens, and inside, the transformation from caterpillar to butterfly begins.

In just nine to fourteen days, the butterfly is completely formed and its orange and black wings can be seen inside the chrysalis. With no visible signs to signal the emergence, the chrysalis cracks open and out tumbles a plump, wet butterfly. As hemolymph is pumped through its body, the butterfly's wings and body expand. About an hour after eclosing, the Monarch will be ready for its first flight. About one month after the egg is laid, a Monarch emerges from its chrysalis. Except for the generation that overwinters in Mexico, most Monarchs live three to four weeks as an adult.

The Metamorphosis of a Baltimore Checkerspot Butterfly

From mid June through late July, female Baltimore Checkerspots lay their tiny yellow eggs on the undersides of Turtlehead *(Chelone)* leaves. The eggs are laid in masses of over a hundred eggs, often with eggs stacked on top of eggs. About two weeks after being laid, the eggs hatch.

Soon after hatching, the caterpillars work together to build a nest around a portion of the Turtlehead plant. Inside the nest they feed communally for the remainder of the summer. When they run out of foliage, they create a new nest to encompass another portion of the plant. On occasion, they might be spotted on the outside of the nest. They too, will molt four times. In fall the caterpillars will leave the plant to overwinter as half grown larvae just below the surface of the soil.

In May, the caterpillars break dormancy and go in search of food. For the remainder of their larval stage, each will feed alone, generally feeding on Turtlehead, Penstemon, or Plantain. During this stage of development, Robins sometimes scoop them up by the mouthful to be fed to their young. Once the caterpillars are full grown, then being around 1-1/2" long, they usually leave their host plant in search of a suitable place to pupate.

A Baltimore Checkerspot chrysalis is absolutely beautiful, white with splendid brown, black, and orange markings. Inside the chrysalis, miraculous changes take place as the caterpillar transforms into a butterfly. Generally, it takes about two weeks for the transformation to occur. Baltimore Checkerspots eclose in the same manner Monarchs do, and then cling to their chrysalis until they are dry and able to fly.

Ten or eleven months after the eggs are laid, Baltimore Checkerspots emerge from their chrysalises to live the remainder of their lives as adults. As an adult, each will live about two weeks.

On cool, cloudy days you will rarely see butterflies in the garden. Until their bodies and flight muscles are warm, they are physically unable to fly.

Part III

Planning the Butterfly Garden

Part III: Planning the Butterfly Garden

Location and Design Considerations

Butterflies are among the most beautiful insects on earth, and one of the few insects we desire to see in our backyard flower gardens. Butterflies don't bite or sting, they assist other insects in the pollination of flowers, and their colorful wings add a decorator's touch to our gardens as they flutter from flower to flower in search of nectar. Attracting an assortment of butterflies to your garden involves essentially two things: (1) planting the right plants in the right place and (2) refraining from the use of insecticides that could be harmful to butterflies. To further increase the number of butterflies that visit the garden, you might incorporate a puddling area (maybe a plastic basin filled with moist sand or soil) or sit a bowl of rotting fruit in or near the garden. With or without these additional lures, however, many butterflies should be enticed to visit a garden that provides desirable plants which are not poisoned with insecticides.

The location of your property plays a role in determining how many butterfly species might visit your garden. Many species prefer open areas while others elect to reside near wet meadows or in deciduous forests. Thus, a person living in an open rural area, near a stream or swamp, and adjacent to a deciduous forest will likely attract more species of butterflies to his or her garden than will an urban gardener.

The best location for a butterfly garden is in full sun. Butterflies are cold-blooded insects that can only fly well when their body and wing muscles are warm. Sunny locations are also advantageous to butterfly eggs and caterpillars, aiding them in more rapid development. And since most of the flowers that attract butterflies for nectar are actually sun-loving plants, all works out quite well in the overall scheme.

Trees, shrubs, or ornamental grasses could serve as a windbreak.

The butterfly garden should be planted in an area that is sheltered from the wind. Wind currents make flight maneuver difficult for butterflies, requiring them to expend extra energy as they attempt to feed, mate, and lay eggs. A windbreak can be provided by simply planting a hedge of evergreens or ornamental grasses to protect the garden from prevailing winds.

You might want to plant your garden where it can be seen from your kitchen or living room window, from a porch or patio, or maybe from the street, where neighbors too might be fascinated by the butterflies you have enticed to come.

Strive for a garden that provides continuous flowering from spring through fall so that butterflies will have nectar available to them for the entire period of time they are in flight. Diligently aim for having lots of flowers in bloom from early July through mid- September since this is when butterflies are most abundant.

Butterflies won't care whether your garden is color coordinated or not—but you might. I personally do not like monochromic gardens, where all of the flowers are different hues of the same color. Nor do I like orange and pink flowers side by side. But people are different. You might

Butterfly Nectar Plants

like a garden that is blanketed in solid yellow if yellow is your favorite color. Or maybe you'd love a garden that is composed entirely of orange and pink flowers planted side by side. Consider your personal preferences and then plan the garden (or gardens) that will suit your own tastes.

When deciding on the plants to incorporate into your butterfly garden, choose a mixture of annuals and perennials. Annuals bloom all summer but must be replanted every spring, after the last frost. Perennials bloom year after year from the same roots but their blooming periods are typically limited to a short period of time, sometimes just a few weeks. To add interest to the garden, mix spiked flowers, daisy-like flowers, and umbel-shaped flower heads. A whole garden of spiked flowers is not as pleasing to the eye as is a garden with assorted-shapes.

So that most of the flowers (and butterflies) in your garden can be seen, plant the shortest flowers in front and the tallest ones in the back. Plant flower species in masses as butterflies seem to choose those flowers that are most abundant. This, of course, could be due to the fact that butterflies can not see detail from a distance. A mass of the same color may draw their attention whereas a single flower or two might not. And surely a massive display of blossoms will emit more scent than just a flower or two.

Most people begin their adventure in butterfly gardening by planting nectar plants for the adult butterflies. As years pass, though, many butterfly gardeners find themselves adding host plants to the landscape. **Host plants** are the plants that butterfly larvae (caterpillars) consume, and they are generally not the same plants that are utilized by adult butterflies as nectar sources. You might think of host plants as butterfly nurseries. With the incorporation of host plants, butterfly numbers (both the number of species and the number of individuals within a species) tend to increase. The correlation between host plant incorporation and increased butterfly numbers is simple, as you will soon learn.

Some experts claim that butterflies prefer pink, lavender, and blue flowers. Others claim they swarm to red, yellow, and orange. I contend that flower color doesn't matter a hoot to a butterfly. Instead, it likely has to do with the composition and concentration of the sugar produced by the plant. Each flower produces a nectar which either lures or deters butterflies from feeding on that particular plant.

*Common Sulphur on Montauk Daisy, top left;
Orange Sulphur on Sedum, top right;
Pearl Crescent on Tropical Milkweed, bottom left;
Spicebush Swallowtail on Butterfly Bush, bottom right.*

Flower color may be of no interest to a butterfly but flower shape certainly matters. If the butterfly can't get its proboscis to where the nectar is, it's obvious that it won't be able to feed on that particular flower. Many flowering plants have been improved through selection and breeding to produce larger flowers, new flower colors, or an abundance of showy flower petals. Often though, the process of breeding changes the composition and concentration of the sugary nectar. Sometimes the process greatly increases the number of petals but dramatically decreases the number of nectaries, the small organs where nectar is produced. If the nectaries are covered with flower petals, butterflies are unable to reach the nectar. This is why single-petaled flowers should usually be chosen over the frilly, doubled types when you are making selections for the butterfly garden.

Different flower shapes also serve to accommodate the different butterfly species. A large butterfly has a long proboscis and is able to reach the nectaries of flowers like daylilies. Small butterflies have short proboscises and cannot probe very deep into flowers. For these species, daisy-like flowers are more suitable.

Both short and tall flowering plants should be incorporated into the garden. Although there are some exceptions, large butterflies tend to feed on towering flowers while small ones generally nectar on the shorter varieties.

Since Part IV of the book illustrates and describes many of the best butterfly nectar plants, I am not going to elaborate on them now. Instead, I will focus here on host plants.

Caterpillar Host Plants

For some butterfly species, its caterpillar can only digest one specific genus of plant foliage. Others are able to consume a number of closely related plants. If a caterpillar is isolated from its host plant, it will die of starvation.

Monarch caterpillars eat Milkweed, and since each female butterfly instinctively knows what her larvae are able to eat, the female Monarch lays her eggs on Milkweed plants. The scientific name for Milkweed is *Asclepias*. Several hundred species of *Asclepias* grow worldwide, with over a hundred species being indigenous to the U.S. Monarch caterpillars have been found feeding on several dozen species of Milkweed in the U.S. and it is assumed that they can safely consume most (or maybe all) Milkweeds.

For every butterfly species that is native to any given area, there is a native plant to host its caterpillars. This means the native host plants are indigenous grasses, plants, shrubs, or trees. Many of the native hosts are plants which we consider weeds. Among the weeds that are used as caterpillar hosts are New England Aster, Turtlehead (*Chelone*), Sweet Violet, Stinging Nettle, Thistle, and Plantain. Amidst the shrubs and trees that are used as hosts are Spicebush, PawPaw, Wild Cherry, Willow, Birch, Poplar, Elm, Hackberry, and Prickly Ash.

Now that I have revealed the fact that many native weeds, trees, and shrubs are butterfly host plants, let me ask that you not attempt to dig up wild plants to transplant onto your property. Most wild flowers do not survive the ordeal of being dug up and then transplanted somewhere else. Some native plants are themselves fighting for survival and becoming scarce as people continue to pluck them from the wild. Instead of taking from the wild, please find a native plant nursery that propagates and sells the plants you are looking for. In the age of the Internet, finding nursery-grown natives is not generally a difficult task.

Since many caterpillar species are able to digest an array of closely related plants, there are domesticated plants that some caterpillars are able to feed on too. The native host plant for Black Swallowtail caterpillars is Wild Carrot (also known as Queen Anne's Lace) but the caterpillars are also able to digest Parsley, Dill, Fennel, and Rue. The

Wild Carrot (also known as Queen Anne's Lace) is one of many weeds that are utilized by butterflies as host plants. Wild Carrot is a host for the Black Swallowtail.

native host plant for Buckeye caterpillars is Plantain, a broadleaf weed that often grows in meadows and lawns, but they can also feed on Snapdragon and Verbena.

Even male butterflies seem to have an innate attraction to the plants that serve as hosts to their particular species. Often I have watched male Monarchs frantically flying over large stands of Milkweed. Even when the Milkweed is in full bloom, they don't stop to nectar, seeming only to be in pursuit of females. I think they inherently know that females might be easy to find in a patch of Milkweed (which they must visit frequently for egg-laying).

Viceroy butterflies most often utilize Willow trees as their host, and Viceroys (males and females) are not often found far from Willow trees. Hackberry Emperors and Tawny Emperors are generally only seen in close proximity to Hackberry trees, which is the host for their larvae.

Hackberry is actually a very good choice of tree to plant if your goal is to attract butterflies for egg-laying. The Tawny Emperor, Hackberry Emperor, Question Mark, Mourning Cloak, and Snout butterfly all utilize Hackberry as a host.

A butterfly's favorite nectar source might lure it in for feeding, but it will not become a permanent resident until both nectar plants and host plants are offered in the same location. Since many adult butterflies live for only a few short weeks, host plants must be readily available for egg laying. They are vital to the survival of the species.

By planting host plants, you will be providing an enormous aid to butterflies, some of which may be in desperate search of host plants. In a world where their natural habitats are being destroyed at a rapid rate, and vast areas of land are being sprayed with insecticides to control Gypsy Moths and mosquitoes, you could be a key sponsor in their survival.

A Table Of Host Plants

This table shows some of the trees, shrubs, perennials, annuals, herbs, and weeds that are often utilized by butterflies as host plants.

Trees and Shrubs that Serve as Caterpillar Hosts

Common Name	Scientific Name	Host For:
Sweet Birch	*Betula lenta*	Tiger Swallowtail, Mourning Cloak, Compton Tortoiseshell
River Birch	*Betula nigra*	Tiger Swallowtail, Mourning Cloak, Compton Tortoiseshell
Gray Birch	*Betula populifolia*	Tiger Swallowtail, Mourning Cloak, Compton Tortoiseshell
Hackberry	*Celtis occidentalis*	Hackberry Emperor, Tawny Emperor, Question Mark, Mourning Cloak, Snout
Tulip Tree	*Liriodendron tulipifera*	Tiger Swallowtail
Quaking Aspen	*Populus tremuloides*	Red-Spotted Purple, White Admiral, Mourning Cloak, Viceroy
Wild Black Cherry	*Prunus serotina*	Tiger Swallowtail, White Admiral, Red-Spotted Purple, Viceroy
Hybrid Elm	*Ulmus hybrids*	Mourning Cloak, Question Mark, Comma
PawPaw	*Asimina triloba*	Zebra Swallowtail

Trees and Shrubs that Serve as Caterpillar Hosts (continued)

Common Name	Scientific Name	Host For:
Weeping Willow	*Salix babylonica*	Viceroy, Mourning Cloak, Tiger Swallowtail, Red-Spotted Purple
Sandbar Willow	*Salix exugia*	Viceroy, Mourning Cloak, Tiger Swallowtail, Red-Spotted Purple
Pussy Willow	*Salix discolor*	Viceroy, Mourning Cloak, Tiger Swallowtail, Red-Spotted Purple
Black Walnut	*Juglans nigra*	Banded Hairstreak
Prickly Ash	*Zanthoxylum americanum*	Giant Swallowtail
Spicebush	*Lindera benzoin*	Spicebush Swallowtail
Sassafras	*Sassafras albidum*	Spicebush Swallowtail

Perennials That Serve As Caterpillar Hosts

Common Name	Scientific Name	Host For:
Swamp Milkweed	*Asclepias incarnata*	Monarch, Queen
Showy Milkweed	*Asclepias speciosa*	Monarch, Queen
Common Milkweed	*Asclepias syriaca*	Monarch, Queen
Butterfly Weed	*Asclepias tuberosa*	Monarch, Queen
New England Aster	*Aster novae-angliae*	Pearl Crescent, Silvery Checkerspot
New York Aster	*Aster novi-belgii*	Pearl Crescent, Silvery Checkerspot
Frikart's Aster	*Aster frikartii*	Orange Sulphur, Clouded Sulphur, Dog Face Sulphur, Eastern Tailed Blue
False Indigo	*Baptisia australis*	Orange Sulphur, Clouded Sulphur, Dog Face Sulphur, Eastern Tailed Blue
Tickseed	*Coreopsis grandiflora*	Buckeye, Silvery Checkerspot, Karner Blue
Lanceleaf Coreopsis	*Coreopsis lanceolata*	Buckeye, Silvery Checkerspot, Karner Blue
Pink Coreopsis	*Coreopsis rosea*	Buckeye, Silvery Checkerspot, Karner Blue
White Turtlehead	*Chelon glabra*	Baltimore Checkerspot
Pink Turtlehead	*Chelone lyonii*	Baltimore Checkerspot
Wild Senna	*Cassia hebecarpa*	Clouded Sulphur, Cloudless Sulphur, Sleepy Orange, Southern Dogface
'Silver Brocade' Artemisia	*Artemisia stelleriana*	Painted Lady, American Lady
Gas Plant	*Dictamnus albus*	Giant Swallowtail

Hops (vine) ....*Humulus lupulus*........................ Question Mark, Comma, Gray Hairstreak

Passion Flower (vine)..................*Passiflora incarnata*................... Gulf Fritillary

Dutchman's Pipe (vine) ....*Aristolochia macrophylla*.......... Pipevine Swallowtail

Annuals That Serve As Caterpillar Hosts

Common Name	Scientific Name	Host For:
Tropical Milkweed	*Asclepias curassavica*	Monarch
Snapdragon	*Antirrhimum*	Buckeye
Spider Flower	*Cleome*	Checkered White
Hollyhock	*Alcea*	Painted Lady, American Lady, Comma
Balsam	*Impatiens balsamina*	American Lady
Nasturtium	*Tropaeolum*	Cabbage White
Cornflower	*Centaurea cyanus*	American Lady

Herbs That Serve As Caterpillar Hosts

Common Name	Scientific Name	Host For:
Dill	*Anethum graveolens*	Black Swallowtail, Anise Swallowtail
Parsley	*Petroselinum*	Black Swallowtail
Fennel	*Foeniculum vulgare*	Black Swallowtail, Anise Swallowtail
Rue	*Ruta graveolens*	Black Swallowtail, Giant Swallowtail
Angelica	*Angelica gigas*	Black Swallowtail, Anise Swallowtail
Comfrey	*Symphytum officinale*	Painted Lady
Borage	*Borago officinalis*	Painted Lady

Weeds That Serve As Caterpillar Hosts

Common Name	Scientific Name	Host For:
Clover	*Trifolium*	Clouded Sulphur, Eastern Tailed Blue, Gray Hairstreak
Stinging Nettle	*Urtica dioica*	Question Mark, Red Admiral
False Nettle	*Boehmeria cylindrical*	Question Mark, Red Admiral
Thistle	*Cirsium*	Painted Lady
Plantain (broadleaf)	*Plantago major*	Buckeye
Pearly Everlasting	*Anaphalis margaritacea*	American Lady

Narrowing the Host Plant Choices

Andy (my husband) and I reside in a rural community that is surrounded by farmlands, meadows, forests, and mountains. Across the road from our house is a large wooded area where Elm, Ash, Maple, Wild Cherry, Tulip Poplar, and Birch trees thrive. Asters and Queen Anne's Lace grow in the nearby meadows and our yard is plentiful with Wild Violets and Plantain because we have never sprayed the lawn to kill off the broadleaf vegetation. Our neighbors have an Apple tree growing in their yard. With all of these wonderful butterfly hosts growing right here, we never had to plant host plants for Tiger Swallowtails, Black Swallowtails, Red-Spotted Purples, Mourning Cloaks, Buckeyes, or Fritillaries.

When I began my venture in butterfly gardening, we had no Milkweed growing on or near our property. Since I wanted Monarchs to become abundant, Tropical Milkweed was the first host plant I incorporated into the garden. Even in its first season, it was utilized by dozens of female Monarchs for egg-laying.

A female Monarch laying an egg on Tropical Milkweed.

The next year I added a cluster of Swamp Milkweed plants to the garden. It too was used as a host for Monarchs. A few years later, a Common Milkweed plant magically appeared in one of our gardens. I was overwhelmed with joy. Andy and I nurtured that weed like it was a prized specimen. The following year, several stalks of Common Milkweed popped up in our yard.

Today, we have dozens of Common Milkweed plants growing sporadically among flowers, grass, and shrubs. We assume that the first plant grew from a seed which might have been dropped into our garden by a bird, or carried here by the wind, and all the others likely sprouted from seeds that were dispersed by the first few plants that bloomed on our property.

Milkweed is generally the first host plant added to butterfly gardens. A few patches of Common Milkweed, Swamp Milkweed, and/or Tropical Milkweed very quickly attract Monarchs for egg-laying. Over the years, Andy and I have found hundreds of Monarch caterpillars in our gardens. From mid July through early October, our property is laden with the orange and black wings of majestic Monarchs.

Before incorporating host plants into your landscape, consider what butterfly species you are likely to attract for egg-laying. It would prove a waste of time and/or money to plant host plants for a butterfly species that has never been spotted in your part of the country. This is where a region-specific field guide would be of value. By knowing what butterflies inhabit your area, you will know what butterflies you might be able to attract.

If a particular butterfly is shown in field guides to reside in or near your area, even if you have never actually seen it, you might try your hand at luring it in by providing one of its host plants. But don't be disappointed if a butterfly appears, colonizes in your area, thrives there for a few years, and then suddenly disappears. Other butterfly gardeners have seen this happen. The reason for the butterfly's disappearance could be that something about the immediate environment has changed, making it difficult for that particular butterfly to survive there.

Before you purchase host plants, survey your neighboring lawns, meadows, fields, and woodlands to see what hosts are already there. Also take note of what butterflies are presently abundant. Generally, when a particular butterfly species is bountiful, it indicates there are already lots of host plants nearby. So instead of planting more hosts for this butterfly, it might be wiser to choose host plants for the butterflies that are scarce.

In nineteen years, I have seen only three or four Zebra Swallowtails in our yard. Maybe they were lost individuals that became disoriented and wandered into our area. Maybe the wind blew them here from Ohio or Virginia, where they are more abundant. All I know is that I love these long-tailed, black and white striped beauties, and I would like to make them permanent residents on our property.

A beautiful Zebra Swallowtail

Pawpaw is the tree on which Zebra Swallowtails lay their eggs, but we have no Pawpaws growing in our area. This past summer, for the first time, I planted a few PawPaw trees. My hope is that a fertilized female eventually passes by here, finds the PawPaw trees, and deposits a few dozen eggs. That may be all it takes to get a colony of Zebra Swallowtails started here. What are the chances of this happening? I really don't know, but the PawPaw trees are planted and waiting.

Reaping The Rewards Of Host Plant Incorporation

Bob Snetsinger, a friend and mentor to me, is a professor of entomology at Penn State University. In 1996 Bob connected with Robert and Elsie Tudek and together they created a butterfly garden at the Tom Tudek Memorial Park in State College, PA.

In 1996, Bob counted just eight species of butterflies in the Tudek Park Butterfly Garden. Since then, Bob, the Tudeks, and others (which eventually included many local Master Gardeners), added numerous nectar plants and host plants to the garden. By 2006, thirty butterfly species resided there. Just ten years after the initial creation of the garden, the number of resident butterfly species had increased by twenty two. And not only did the number of butterfly species increase but so too did the number of butterflies within a species. Bob attributes the greatest gain to the incorporation of host plants.

By planting butterfly host plants, you are actually incorporating butterfly nurseries into your garden. You are doing more than just luring the butterflies in; you are virtually ensuring that the local population will multiply.

In June of 2008, a helicopter sprayed Bt on a wooded area just north of Tudek Park. Wind blew a heavy drift of Bt into the butterfly garden. As a result, the caterpillars of most butterfly species were killed and the butterfly numbers dwindled to dramatically low counts. By 2011, three years after the garden was drenched with Bt, the butterfly population in Tudek Park was on the rebound but still the butterfly count was much lower than it was in 2007.

On Behalf of All Butterflies

Monarch butterflies are fortunate in having numerous organizations hard at work in studying their biology, monitoring their population status, and educating the public on the struggles of their survival. Among these are Monarch Watch, The Monarch Program, Monarch Butterfly Fund, Monarch Lab, Monarch Monitoring Project, Southwest Monarch Study, and Monarch Joint Venture.

The Monarch-oriented organizations have assuredly aided the Monarch in its quest to survive. Gardeners, and even elementary school students, are now being educated on the needs of this butterfly. Many people are able to identify a Monarch when they see one, they know that Monarchs over-winter in Mexico and that their Mexican habitat must be protected, and that females lay their eggs on Milkweed.

Thousands of people have planted Milkweed. In the last five years, Milkweed sales have nearly doubled on my website. Milkweeds are now, by far, my top selling plants.

Only the Monarch can boast of having such a huge following of supporters devoted to its survival. Most U.S. residents cannot distinguish a Tiger Swallowtail from a Giant Swallowtail, they have no idea what plants are utilized as hosts by either of these two beautiful butterflies, and they haven't a clue as to where or how they over-winter. While both the Tiger Swallowtail and the Giant Swallowtail populations are dwindling in number too, maybe partly due to the aerial spraying of insecticides to reduce the Gypsy Moth and mosquito populations, few people are doing anything to help them.

While I am thrilled to see people joining together to assist Monarchs in their fight to survive, I am saddened by the thought that other butterfly species are dwindling in number too, while few people are stepping in to help them.

Baltimore Checkerspot butterflies used to be abundant in this area. In mid-May, I could easily count fifty or more caterpillars on the Turtlehead and Penstemon plants in my butterfly garden. By late June, the garden was alive with the bright colored wings of Baltimore Checkerspots. But that was ten years ago. Today, there are none. From abundant to none in ten short years!

I wish I could say it is only in my back yard from which Baltimores have disappeared, but this is not the case. Numerous butterfly gardeners in Pennsylvania and surrounding states have reported that their Baltimore populations have vanished too.

I even wish I could say it is only the Baltimore that is rapidly declining in number in central Pennsylvania, but it is not. Bob Snetsinger, the butterfly expert at Penn State University, has seen a decline in butterfly numbers at several locations where he has been counting them from summer to summer for the past sixteen years. A few years ago Bob saw no Giant Swallowtails one summer and feared they had been wiped out by Bt spraying and/or the destruction of natural habitat. But then, to his surprise, they reappeared in diminished numbers two summers later.

Giant Swallowtails are large, beautiful, graceful butterflies. (Flip to page 51 to see a few photos of them.) When they glide down into the garden from atop tall trees in the woods, it is a spectacular sight. For these magnificent long-tailed, yellow and black beauties to survive, they need only water, nectar plants and host plants that are insecticide-free, and air that is safe to breathe. The males require moist soil from which to extract salts and other nutrients.

In Florida, Giant Swallowtails lay their eggs on Citrus trees while further north, the eggs are generally laid on Prickly Ash. But Giant Swallowtails will also utilize Rue *(Ruta graveolens)* as a host plant. Used by both the Giant Swallowtail and the Black Swallowtail as a host, Rue is handsome, easy to grow, and relatively insect free (except for the appearance of Swallowtail caterpillars). But how many people have planted Rue? Very few.

Hackberry, Quaking Aspen, Wild Cherry, and Willow trees each serve as a host to three or more butterfly species. Hops, a vine whose "cones" are used in beer making, serves as a host to Question Mark, Comma, and Gray Hairstreak butterflies. Dill and Fennel are hosts for Black Swallowtails in eastern states and Anise Swallowtails in the West.

Host plants are vital to the survival of every butterfly species. Milkweed will aid the Monarch in its quest to survive, but it will not serve as a host plant for other butterfly species. To help the other beautiful butterflies, we must plant host plants for them too.

Part IV

The Best-Of-The-Best Butterfly-Attracting Plants

Part IV: The Best-of-the-Best Butterfly-Attracting Plants

Why The Disagreement?

If you have read other books and articles on butterfly gardening, you have likely noticed that authors don't always agree on which flowers work best to attract butterflies. One author proclaims Pentas, Lantana, and Black-eyed Susans to be the very best nectar plants while another insists they are not even in the top ten. I think there are logical explanations for the lack of consensus. One reason for disagreement stems from the fact that different authors reside in different parts of the U.S., while likewise, different butterfly species dwell in different regions too. Some of the native southern butterflies may like Pentas and Lantanas whereas most of the northern butterflies may not. It could even be the case that northern soils don't produce the same sweet nectar that is produced when Pentas and Lantanas are grown in the South.

Some butterfly gardeners are native plant enthusiasts and advocate strict adherence to planting indigenous plants in the butterfly garden. Thus, their lists of the best butterfly attracting plants will include only natives. Native plant gardeners generally rank Yarrow and Goldenrod quite high on their lists. And I agree that these two are highly sought out in the wild, as I often I see butterflies nectaring on Yarrow and Goldenrod as I am driving along the highway. When these plants are offered alongside Butterfly Bush, though, they quickly lose their popularity with butterflies. Observing activity in our yard, I very seldom see a butterfly on either Yarrow or Goldenrod.

I am not a native-only gardener. I understand that indigenous plants do better in the landscape because they have evolved to withstand the elements of the local environment; but, still, I yearn for some of the exotic plants which are offered to gardeners. I even think the butterflies appreciate the fact that I am not a native-only gardener for if I were, they would be deprived of Butterfly Bush, Tropical Milkweed, Mexican Sunflower, and Zinnia, four of their favorite nectar sources. While many of the plants in my gardens are actually natives, they are not there *because* they are native plants. They are there because I find those particular plants desirable—and so too do the butterflies.

Another factor to consider in the discrepancy over what flowers best attract butterflies has to do with the fact that no two authors are rating the exact same palate of plants. While many butterfly gardens include some of the same plant species, other plant species are unique to just a few gardens. With different authors rating different plants, it's obvious their best-of-the-best plant lists will be different also. When a top notch nectar source is not even among those being ranked by a specific author, it will not be included on that author's list.

Even the species or cultivar of plant which is tested can make a huge difference. I planted *Liatris spicata* (known as Kansas Gayfeather or Blazing Star) in my first butterfly garden because numerous authors recommended it. Butterflies rarely nectared on this species. Recently, I incorporated *Liatris ligustylis* (commonly called Rocky Mountain Blazing Star) into the garden and found that butterflies, especially Monarchs, love it. 'Norah Leigh' Garden Phlox (*Phlox paniculata* 'Norah Leigh') does not attract many butterflies whereas 'Jeana' Garden Phlox (*Phlox paniculata* 'Jeana') is a butterfly magnet.

How I Choose the Best-Of-The-Best

Over the years I found that some flowers attract certain species of butterflies but not others, and some butterfly species seldom nectar on some of the plants that most other species seem to love. I'm sure this was Mother Nature's intention. It probably wouldn't have worked out too well if all the butterflies of the world craved the nectar of just twelve plants.

I was not in a hurry to compile my list of the best butterfly-attracting plants. Not until now, after nineteen years of avid, intense butterfly gardening, and experimentation with a few hundred annual and perennial plant species, have I compiled it. In presenting my list of the best butterfly-attracting plants, I must emphasize that some of these plants may prove to be wonderful butterfly lures for the northeastern gardener but rather worthless in the southern and western states (where there are many different butterfly species that we don't have here in Pennsylvania). I do think, though, that even in other regions, some butterflies will nectar on most of the plants I advocate in this book.

I will present my best-of-the-best butterfly attracting plants in the order in which I rank their attractiveness to butterflies. While most of the featured plants function strictly as nectar plants, a few (like Brazilian Verbena and the plants in the Milkweed family) are utilized as both nectar and host plants. The last two plants illustrated, *Artemisia* 'Silver Brocade' and Rue, are used only as host plants, but both deserve a place in every butterfly garden. American Lady and Painted Lady butterflies readily deposit their eggs on *Artemisia* 'Silver Brocade', even when there is Thistle, Pearly Everlasting, and Hollyhock (their well known hosts) near by. Rue, serving as a host to both Black Swallowtails and Giant Swallowtails, makes a lovely garden specimen.

The plants I highly recommend for the butterfly garden are:

1. **Butterfly Bush**
2. **Purple Coneflower**
3. **Garden Phlox 'Jeanna'**
4. **Tropical Milkweed**
5. **Swamp Milkweed**
6. **Common Milkweed**
7. **Butterfly Weed**
8. **Meadow Blazing Star**
9. **Coreopsis 'Early Sunrise'**
10. **Zinnia**
11. **Brazilian Verbena**
12. **Mexican Sunflower**
13. **Scabiosa 'Butterfly Blue'**
14. **Joe-Pye Weed**
15. **Cosmos**
16. **Verbena 'Homestead Purple'**
17. **Sedum 'Autunm Joy'**
18. **Lilac**
19. **Artemisia 'Silver Brocade'**
20. **Rue**

Now let's take a look at each of these plants.

Butterfly Bush

Buddleia davidii or Buddleja davidii

Mature Height: 5' – 8'

USDA Plant Hardiness Zones: 5 – 9

Light Requirements: Full sun or part shade

Bloom Time: July thru frost

Butterfly Bushes, which are sometimes called Summer Lilacs, are native to China. They generally grow 5' to 8' high and 4' to 5' wide. Most are delightfully fragrant, smelling somewhat like the spring-blooming Lilac. All are perennial shrubs which grow well in average garden soil and are hardy in zones 5 – 9.

Butterfly Bushes are available in white, pink, lavender, purple, yellow, and blue-flowering cultivars. 'White Profusion' and 'Pink Profusion' produce the largest flower spikes and both are attractive to butterflies, as are all of the other cultivars, with the exception of yellow-flowering cultivars.

'Attraction', 'Harlequin', and 'Royal Red' all produce beautiful magenta colored flowers. 'Black Knight' yields deep navy-blue flower spikes. 'Butterfly Heaven', 'Lochinch', and 'Dartmoor' are among the Butterfly Bush cultivars that bear lavender blooms. 'Cornwall Blue' produces spikes that are as close to true blue as you can find in a Butterfly Bush.

In recent years, some shorter growing cultivars have been introduced. Among them are 'Peacock' (which yields large, pinkish lavender blooms) and 'Adonis Blue' (which yields fragrant deep blue flower spikes). While these cultivars are still difficult to find, they may be worth the effort if you need a Butterfly Bush that is shorter than most.

Butterfly Bushes are appropriately named, for they generally attract more butterflies than any other plant. Among the butterflies that are attracted to Butterfly Bushes are Monarchs, Swallowtails, Fritillaries, Viceroys, Sulphurs, Red Admirals, Painted Ladies, Buckeyes, and more. Butterfly Bushes also attract hummingbirds, hummingbird moths, and bees.

Butterfly Bushes are generally easy-care shrubs. They should be cut back to about 36" in late fall, around the end of November. If you don't get them trimmed back in fall, however, you may still do so the next spring.

Sometimes Butterfly Bushes die to the ground over winter. But even when you fear they have died, they usually sprout new growth in June and quickly grow to become large shrubs again, often that same year.

It is wise to deadhead Butterfly Bushes (cut off the spent blossoms) as this will encourage new buds to form. Deadheading also serves to slightly increase the size of oncoming flower spikes (though always the first show of flowers will include the largest spikes).

Note: The yellow-flowering Butterfly Bushes *(Buddleia x weyeriana* 'Honeycomb' *and Buddleia x weyeriana* 'Sungold'*)* do not attract very many butterflies. Being of a different species *(B. weyeriana, not B. davidii)*, these bushes must not produce a nectar that is pleasing to the tastes of butterflies.

Purple Coneflower

Echinacea purpurea

Mature Height: 30" – 36"

USDA Plant Hardiness Zones: 4 – 9

Light Requirements: Full sun or part shade

Bloom Time: July – frost

Purple Coneflower, one of my favorite perennials, is also one of the butterflies' favorite flowers. This plant is native to the central plains and eastern woodlands of the U.S. Wild Purple Coneflowers have small lavender-pink flowers with drooping petals and look rather sickly compared to the beautiful cultivars on the market today. Plant selection and breeding have greatly enhanced the beauty—and the demand—for this stately perennial. Most of the new cultivars have large flowers (up to 5" across) with petals that stand straight out (horizontally) rather than droop. Most have deep, rich, lavender-pink to bright pink flowers.

Among the wonderful cultivars available are 'Bright Star', 'Ruby Star', 'Crimson Star', and Magnus'. All seem to attract butterflies equally well. Among the butterflies that are attracted to Purple Coneflower are Monarchs, Fritillaries, Sulphurs, and Swallowtails.

Purple Coneflower is easy to grow and will spread rapidly if you allow it to self sow. It is quite hardy, drought tolerant, and rarely bothered by insect pests or disease.

In just the last few years, plant breeders have developed a lot of exciting, new Coneflowers. Many of the newcomers can't technically be called *purple* Coneflowers, though, because some bear flowers that are yellow, orange, green, or white. 'Sunrise' and 'Harvest Moon' yield yellow daisies while 'Sundown' and 'Hot Summer' produce orange ones. 'Solar Flare', one of my favorites, is adorned with huge, orange-red daisy-like flowers with dark centers. 'Green Jewel' and 'Green Envy' bear greenish-white daisies while 'Virgin' and 'Avalanche' deliver bright, brilliant white ones.

Of the many new other-than-purple cultivars, I only have 'Harvest Moon' (yellow-flowering) 'Sundown' (orange-flowering), and 'Solar Flare' (orange-red flowers) planted in my garden. Each attracts butterflies but not nearly as many as do the purple-pink varieties. For the beginning butterfly gardener, my recommendation would be to resist the newer yellow, orange, green, and white cultivars in favor of the more traditional lavender-pink.

> Remember: You should plant flower species in mass rather than place individual plants sporadically throughout the garden. Keep in mind, too, that some perennials multiply rapidly (either by root or by reseeding) and, therefore, should not be planted too closely together.

Garden Phlox 'Jeana'

Phlox paniculata 'Jeana'

Mature Height: 30" – 36"

USDA Plant Hardiness Zones: 4 – 8

Light Requirements: Full sun or part shade

Bloom Time: July – September

Over the years, I have presented numerous cultivars of Garden Phlox to the butterflies in my vicinity. Not until I finally found 'Jeana', though, was I impressed by the ability of a Garden Phlox to lure butterflies. Butterflies absolutely love 'Jeana'.

Founded by and named after Jeana Prewitt of Nashville, TN, this selection of native Phlox possesses outstanding mildew resistance as compared to most. Its tennis ball-shaped flower heads are lavender-pink and highly fragrant.

Swallowtails are especially drawn to Phlox 'Jeana' but Monarchs and Fritillaries like it too. Because of its popularity with butterflies, I suggest you plant several of this particular cultivar in your garden.

Like most Garden Phlox, 'Jeana' is easy to grow in average garden soil. Its also a long bloomer, producing flower heads from mid-July thru September. It might not be an easy perennial to find though. 'Jeana' is a relatively new introduction which produces smaller flowers than most Garden Phlox do, so it will likely take a few years for it to saturate the market.

Hummingbird Clearwing Moth (*Hemaris thysbe*)

Sometimes mistaken for baby hummingbirds or large bumblebees, Hummingbird Clearwing Moths are daytime flyers which frequently nectar at Butterfly Bush, Beebalm, Phlox, and Verbena 'Homestead Purple'. Just like hummingbirds, they hover in mid air as they feed. They lay their eggs on Viburnum and Honeysuckle.

Tropical Milkweed

Asclepias curassavica

Mature Height: 30" – 40"

Annual

Light Required: Full sun or part shade

Tropical Milkweed, also known as Bloodflower and Mexican Milkweed, is believed to be a native of South America. Being of tropical descent, it must be treated as an annual in most of the United States.

Like most Milkweeds, Tropical Milkweed secretes a milk-like sap when a stem or leaf is broken. And like many Milkweeds, its tiny, star-shaped blossoms are borne in rounded clusters. Its flowers may be yellow, orange, or red, and often the flowers are bi-colored. 'Silky Yellow' is a cultivar that produces yellow flowers, while 'Silky Red' yields festive yellow/red bi-colored blooms.

Tropical Milkweed is most often propagated from seed and is an easy plant to grow in any average garden soil. If seeds are sown indoors around mid-March and then the transplants set into the garden after the last spring frost, the plants should grow quickly and begin to bloom around mid-July. From then until frost, Tropical Milkweed will flower profusely.

When Tropical Milkweed is blooming it attracts many butterflies for nectar. Among these are Monarchs, Fritillaries, Pearl Crescents, and Red Admirals.

Whether the plants are blooming or not, they will lure female Monarchs in for egg-laying. When the females have before them a smorgasbord of Milkweed species, they will almost always choose the Tropical Milkweed for depositing their eggs.

Maybe the females choose this species because the leaves are so tender, thus being easy for their tiny caterpillar hatchlings to bite off and chew. Or maybe Monarchs sense, by tapping their feet on the leaves to taste it, that this particular Milkweed species contains the perfect amount of toxic substance to make her offspring exceptionally distasteful to birds. I don't really know why Monarchs tend to prefer Tropical Milkweed for egg-laying, but, for sure, they do.

Once you have Tropical Milkweed growing in your garden, you can collect its seeds for sowing the following spring. The seeds will be inside elongated seed pods. I suggest you don't collect the seed pods before they begin to split open on their own. Only then can you be sure that the seeds are mature enough to harvest. Remove the seeds from the seed pod and discard the empty pods and all of the white fluff. Allow the seeds to dry and then place them in a small plastic bag. Keep the bag of seeds in a cool, dark place until you are ready to plant them the next spring. If you have space in your refrigerator, that is a great place for storing seeds. To my husband's dismay, I have claimed the entire vegetable bin in our refrigerator for storing the many seeds I collect every fall.

Note: If you get Tropical Milkweed sap on your hands, immediately wash it off with warm, soapy water. Do not touch your face with your hands until the sap has been washed off. This milky sap can cause great discomfort if it comes into contact with your eyes.

Swamp Milkweed

Asclepias incarnata

Mature Height: 30" – 48"

USDA Plant Hardiness Zones: 3 – 9

Light Requirements: Full sun or part shade

Bloom Time: Late June thru July

Swamp Milkweed is another top choice for the butterfly garden. It is indigenous to the U.S. and its native range includes the eastern and central states. In its native environment, Swamp Milkweed usually grows in moist locations (like in swamps or along the banks of rivers, streams, or ponds).

Swamp Milkweed generally blooms for about three weeks beginning the end of June. When it is blooming, butterflies abound. Among the butterfly species that are attracted to Swamp Milkweed for nectar are Monarchs, Swallowtails, Fritillaries, Red-Spotted Purples, Painted Ladies, and Red Admirals.

Swamp Milkweed is available in pink-flowering and white-flowering cultivars. 'Cinderella' and 'Soulmate' produce pink flowers while 'Ice Ballet' and 'Ice Follies' yield white. Butterflies seem to be attracted equally well to both the pink- and white-flowering cultivars.

Swamp Milkweed is relatively easy to grow from seed, but seeds may be difficult to find. I recommend planting the seeds outdoors in spring after the last frost. Once the plants reach a height of about 6", transplant them into the garden, spacing them at least 20" apart. Each plant will likely have just one stem in its first year of growth, and it will not likely bloom. In subsequent years, however, each plant will bush out as three to eight stems shoot up from the roots. In its second year of growth, the plant should yield flowers.

I have found Swamp Milkweed to be a rather short-lived perennial, growing beautifully for three to five years, and then simply disappearing. Generally, though, new plants will appear in its place as reseeding is pretty common.

While Swamp Milkweed grows natively in moist locations, it also does just fine in drier soils. In drier soils, in periods of severe drought, water it well once a week and the plant will be satisfied.

Swamp Milkweed is another Milkweed species that is highly utilized by female Monarchs for egg-laying. It tends to be their second choice of Milkweed species, and a close contender for their first choice, which is Tropical Milkweed. Its leaves, too, are quite tender and, thus, easy for tiny caterpillars to bite off and chew.

Tiger Swallowtail on Swamp Milkweed.

Common Milkweed

Asclepias syriaca

Mature Height: 40" – 50"

USDA Plant Hardiness Zones: 3– 8

Light Requirements: Full sun or part shade

Bloom Time: Late June thru July

Common Milkweed is also a U.S. native. Its distribution range includes the eastern half of the United States (with the exception of Florida) and most of Canada. Common Milkweed produces large clusters of mauve-pink flowers which have a sweet-smelling fragrance.

Common Milkweed spreads from its roots and can, according to some people, become invasive. Ask me about this, though, and I'll say that it simply becomes abundant. I adore Common Milkweed, so much so that my husband very carefully mows around it when it sporadically pops up in our yard. Unless he doesn't want dinner, he knows to leave the Milkweed alone.

Common Milkweed usually blooms late June thru July and when it is blooming, butterflies readily appear to feed on its tasty nectar. Among the butterflies that utilize this plant as a nectar source are Monarchs, Swallowtails, and most other butterfly species, including Hairstreaks, which you will almost always find on Common Milkweed when it is in bloom.

Very few nurseries (other than native plant nurseries) offer Common Milkweed. To many nurseries this plant is nothing more than a common weed, and why would they want to offer weeds? To avid butterfly gardeners, though, Common Milkweed is a highly sought prize.

If you wish to incorporate Common Milkweed into your butterfly garden (or maybe plant it somewhere it can spread without interfering with other highly prized plants) but are unable to find plants, you might try growing it from seed. In suggesting this, however, I must say that it is not easy to grow from seed. Only as a last resort should propagation by seed be considered.

Common Milkweed is utilized by Monarchs for egg-laying, but if Tropical Milkweed or Swamp Milkweed is available to the gravid females, they will most often choose one of these in lieu of the Common. In open fields and pastures where other Milkweed species are not available, the females readily lay their eggs on Common Milkweed.

Common Milkweed flower, closeup

Common Milkweed seed pods

Butterfly Weed

Asclepias tuberosa

Mature Height: 18" – 30"

USDA Plant Hardiness Zones: 4 – 9

Light Requirements: Full sun or part shade

Bloom Time: Late June thru July

Another Milkweed species, Butterfly Weed is a U.S. native with its distribution range being the eastern and central states. In its native surroundings, it usually grows along roadsides and in meadows and prairies. Wherever you see it, you can suspect that the soil is well-draining and somewhat sandy. In heavy, rich soils, this plant generally does not survive.

Butterfly Weed grows in dense clumps and produces rounded clusters of tiny, bright orange flowers. It usually blooms from late June thru July and when it is in bloom, butterflies of many species converge on it.

In recent years a few new flower colors have been introduced. Among these are yellow and red (which I have yet to see). 'Hello Yellow', of course, yields yellow blooms and 'Gay Butterflies' is supposed to produce flowers that are either yellow, orange, or red. While I have been in search for a red-flowering Butterfly Weed for many years, I have not yet found one. They must be extremely rare.

Butterfly Weed can be started from seed but they are not easy to grow from seed. For this reason I suggest you, instead, purchase a plant wherever you can find one. Then, once you have found a plant, place it in the garden where you are sure you want it to grow. Butterfly Weeds produce long tap roots, and once established, they are quite difficult to transplant.

Monarch butterflies only rarely utilize this plant for egg-laying, that is, so long as Tropical Milkweed, Swamp Milkweed, or Common Milkweed are in the vicinity. Maybe female Monarchs don't readily choose this plant for egg deposit because it has thin, tough, bristle-like leaves which would be difficult for tiny caterpillars to chew.

If this plant flowered longer or was utilized more often as a Monarch host plant, I would have ranked it higher on my best-of-the-best list. In my opinion, however, it belongs where I have put it, at number 7 on the list.

Along with Monarch caterpillars, you may see these insects on your Milkweed plants too:

Oleander Aphid    **Milkweed Tussock Moth**    **Milkweed Bug**

Meadow Blazing Star

Liatris ligulistylis

Mature Height: 30" – 36"

USDA Plant Hardiness Zones: 3 – 9

Light Requirements: Full sun or part shade

Bloom Time: Late July thru August

Meadow Blazing Star, also known as Rocky Mountain Blazing Star and Meadow Gayfeather, is a U.S. native that grows in the plains and prairies of the western half of the country. It is an easy-to-grow perennial, asking only to be watered occasionally in periods of prolonged drought.

Many perennial gardeners are familiar with another Liatris species, *Liatris spicata*, commonly called Gayfeather or Blazing Star. Gayfeather produces beautiful, florist-quality flower spikes, but the flowers are only rarely utilized by butterflies as a nectar source. Meadow Blazing Star is different, it being absolutely irresistible to Monarchs and at least moderately attractive to several other butterfly species.

If you are looking for a wonderful cut flower, select *Liatris spicata*. But if you are looking for the Monarch magnet, *Liatris ligulistylis* is the species you should incorporate into the garden.

Oleander Aphid *(Aphis nerii)*
Oleander Aphids, also known as Milkweed Aphids, begin to appear on Milkweed plants toward the end of summer. Their numbers quickly multiply to the point where the upper portion of the Milkweed stem might be covered with these tiny, bright yellow insects. Aphids suck juice from the host plant and secrete a 'honeydew' which attracts ants for feeding. The honeydew sometimes develops to be an unsightly, black, mold-like substance, too. Because Oleander Aphids suck life-sustaining juice from Milkweed and secrete honeydew which attract ants (which feed not only on the honeydew but also on Monarch eggs and caterpillars), I rid my plants of Aphids on a regular basis. What I have found to work well for reducing Aphid numbers is to pinch the infested stems and leaves with my fingers to kill the Aphids. Then, I rinse the dead from the plants with a spray of water from the garden hose. By doing this every five to seven days, the Aphid population remains minimal.

Milkweed Tussock Moth Caterpillar
(Euchaetes egle)
Tussock Moths lay their eggs in mass on Milkweed leaves. When the eggs hatch, the caterpillars feed communally for at least the first half of their larval stage. In the early instars the caterpillars appear white, gray, or greenish. The more mature caterpillars look like the colorful, hairy one pictured to the left. In large numbers, the larvae can defoliate Milkweed plants. Adult Milkweed Tussock Moths are drab gray with yellowish abdomens.

Milkweed Bug *(Oncopeltus fasciatus)*
Milkweed Bugs reside in states lying east of the Rocky Mountains. Mature adults are orange with black spots. Freshly molted individuals are pale yellow with gray spots. Milkweed Bugs feed predominately on the juice and seeds of Milkweed. There are several other species of orange-colored Milkweed bugs and beetles that also feed on Milkweed. You might want to explore the Internet for information about those.

Coreopsis 'Early Sunrise'

Coreopsis grandiflora 'Early Sunrise'

Mature Height: 16" – 20"

USDA Plant Hardiness Zones: 4 – 9

Light Requirements: Full sun or part shade

Bloom Time: June – frost

There are many Coreopsis species and cultivars on the market but I doubt any would bloom longer or attract more butterflies than 'Early Sunrise'. Coreopsis 'Early Sunrise' usually begins to bloom around mid June and it doesn't stop until mid September. And all summer long butterflies visit its flowers for nectar.

The bright yellow, daisy-like flowers of 'Early Sunrise' are only about 2" in diameter but a mature plant can produce well over two hundred flowers each summer. The butterflies attracted to 'Early Sunrise' include Fritillaries, Red Admirals, American Ladies, Painted Ladies, Baltimore Checkerspots, and more.

'Early Sunrise' Coreopsis is easy to grow and can be started from seed. From seed, though, it will not likely bloom until the second year. If your preference is to purchase a plant, this plant shouldn't be hard to find. Most perennial nurseries keep it in stock all summer long.

To keep the plant looking neat and tidy, you might want to periodically deadhead it (remove the spent flowers). Other than that, you will find 'Early Sunrise' Coreopsis to be an exceptionally easy-care plant. Almost never is it bothered by plant pests or disease.

This plant readily reseeds and can become invasive. To prevent this from happening, be diligent in removing the spent blooms.

2012 USDA Plant Hardiness Zone Map

In 2012, the U.S. Department of Agriculture released a new version of its Plant Hardiness Zone Map. Compared to the last version (the map released in 1990), the 2012 map shows slight shifts in zone boundaries in many areas.

To determine what zone you live in, pinpoint your location on the map to the right. Then match its color to the color on the key. This will tell you what hardiness zone you live in.

The temperatures shown on the key reflect the Average Annual Extreme Minimum Temperature over a 30-year period, 1976 - 2005.

Temp (F)	Zone
-40 to -30	3
-30 to -20	4
-20 to -10	5
-10 to 0	6
0 to 10	7
10 to 20	8
20 to 30	9
30 to 40	10
40 to 50	11

Zinnia

Zinnia elegans or *Z. angustifolia*

Mature Height: 8" – 48"

Annual.

Light Requirements: Full sun or part shade

Bloom Time: July thru frost

Zinnias are annuals. You can either start them from seed or purchase ready-grown plants at a nursery. If you are purchasing from a nursery, make sure they have not been treated with insecticides that might poison butterflies.

Zinnias are available in many sizes, types, and colors. For the butterfly garden, the best choices are the single-bloom types, not the frilly-petal, pom-pom types. You can choose any species that grows 12" to 48" high. Since Zinnias are generally a favorite with butterflies, I suggest you plant several varieties, choosing different heights and flower colors. Smaller butterflies tend to nectar on the shorter zinnias while larger ones nectar most often on the taller cultivars.

In my garden, I have had success attracting butterflies with Zinnia 'Profusion' (which grow 12" to 15" high), Zinnia 'Zowie Yellow Flame' (which grows to around 28" high and yields gorgeous yellow/red bi-colored flowers), Zinnia 'Dahlia-Flowered Mix' (which grows to 36" high), and Zinnia 'State Fair' (which grows to 36" high). But I am sure that other cultivars will attract butterflies too.

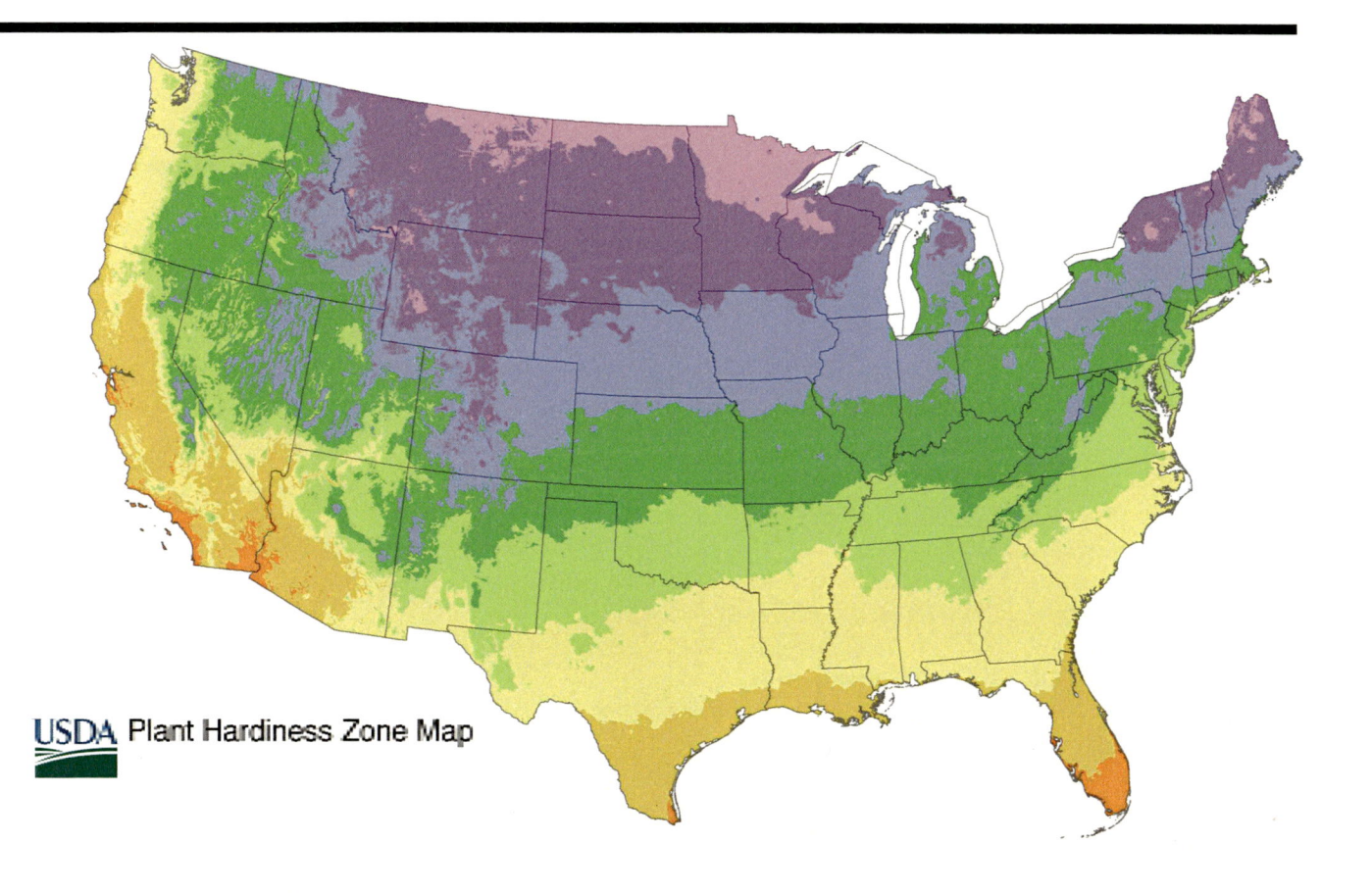

USDA Plant Hardiness Zone Map

Brazilian Verbena

Verbena bonariensis

Mature Height: 30" – 36"

USDA Plant Hardiness Zones: 7 – 9

Light Requirements: Full sun preferred

Bloom Time: July – frost

    Brazilian Verbena grows tall but it doesn't necessarily have to be planted near the back of the butterfly garden. Since you can see right through its tall, airy stems, it can be planted a little closer to the front.

    Brazilian Verbena blooms from mid-July through frost, yielding clusters of tiny lavender-violet flowers. Among the butterflies attracted to it are Cabbage Whites, Sulphurs, and Monarchs.

    Although it is only hardy to zone 7, it almost always reseeds, making it a permanent resident of the garden. To be assured of having this plant from year to year, collect some seeds every fall. That way, if it doesn't reseed on its own, you will have fresh seed to sow. Plant the seeds outdoors in early May and they will likely be blooming by late July.

    Aside from being utilized as a nectar source, Brazilian Verbena is sometimes used as a host plant by Common Buckeyes.

Mexican Sunflower

Tithonia rotundifolia

Mature Height: 36" – 48"

Annual

Light Requirements: Full sun preferred

Bloom Time: July – frost

    Mexican Sunflower is an annual. Not generally available as ready-grown plants, you usually must resort to purchasing seeds that you will sow yourself.

    Mexican Sunflowers generate bright orange daisy-like flowers from late July through frost (so long as the seed is sown by mid-May). Its blooms attract Monarchs, Fritillaries, Sulphurs, and more for nectar.

    There are several cultivars of Tithonia (Mexican Sunflower) that are commonly sold as seed. 'Fiesta del Sol' produces 2" to 3" blooms on plants that grow to around 30" high, while 'Sundance' and 'Torch' yield 3" to 4" blooms and grow 30" to 48" high.

    In my opinion, this is a plant that should be in every butterfly garden. Its rich orange color adds vibrant color while visiting butterflies add lively sparkle.

Scabiosa 'Butterfy Blue'

Scabiosa columbara 'Butterfly Blue'

Mature Height: 15" – 20"

USDA Plant Hardiness Zones: 6 – 9

Light Requirements: Full sun or part shade

Bloom Time: June – September

'Butterfly Blue' Scabiosa was first introduced in the mid 1990s and since then it has become one of the best selling perennials of all time. It blooms from early June (or earlier) until late September (or later). Its small but numerous lavender-blue blooms are butterfly magnets wherever butterflies abound. Because this plant tends to bloom longer into fall than most others do, it is certainly worth having.

To keep this plant looking its best, it should be deadheaded on a regular basis, say every two weeks or so. Whether it is deadheaded or not, it will bloom from spring through fall. 'Butterfly Blue' is easy to grow and only rarely bothered by insect pests or disease.

While many nurserymen claim that this plant is hardy to zone 4, I somewhat doubt that. Having lost numerous 'Butterfly Blue' Scabiosas in harsh Pennsylvania winters, I think it may only be hardy to zone 6 or so.

Because this plant is a sterile hybrid, it cannot be started from seed. *Scabiosa columbaria* 'Nana' looks almost identical to 'Butterfly Blue' and can be grown from seed, but it only blooms for about six weeks.

Joe-Pye Weed

Eupatorium purpureum

Mature Height: 48" – 60"

USDA Plant Hardiness Zones: 3 – 9

Light Requirements: Full or part sun

Bloom Time: July – August

Joe-Pye Weed is native to the U.S. Its distribution range includes the eastern half of the U.S. Generally, it is found growing along streams or in other locations where the soil tends to stay rather moist.

Joe-Pye Weed grows quickly to become a bold, tall, stately plant. Then in July or August, it produces gigantic umbels of tiny, fuzzy mauve-pink flowers.

Joe-Pye Weed might be hard to find anywhere other than in a native plant nursery. It's another one of those natives that are overlooked as flowers and treated simply as weeds.

If you would like to plant a shorter Joe-Pye Weed, I suggest you look for 'Little Joe' (*Eupatorium dubium* 'Little Joe') or 'Phantom' (*Eupatorium maculatum* 'Phantom'), both of which mature at 36" to 48" high. Their flowers are much smaller than those of the native species but the flowers are nonetheless utilized by butterflies as a nectar source.

Cosmos

Cosmos bipennatus or *C. sulphureus*

Mature Height: 18" – 36"

Annual.

Light Requirements: Full or part sun

Bloom Time: July thru frost

Cosmos are annuals that love the sun, are quite drought tolerant, and are rarely bothered by insect pests or disease. They are available in white, pink, lavender, yellow, and orange-blooming varieties. Cosmos can generally be purchased at greenhouses and nurseries but they can also be started from seed.

Cosmos are easy to grow. Just give them an average garden soil and a sunny location and they will reward you with an abundance of bright, cheery flowers from mid-July through frost. Sometimes they will reseed.

There are many cultivars available. 'Cosmic' is a dwarf that grows 12" to 18" high and produces yellow, orange, or scarlet blossoms. 'Sonata' matures at 20" to 28" tall and yields rose, white, or pink flowers. 'Bright Lights' towers at 30" to 36" high and bears yellow, orange, or scarlet blooms.

The butterflies attracted to Cosmos include Fritillaries, Swallowtails, Sulphurs, and Ladies.

Verbena 'Homestead Purple'

Verbena canadensis 'Homestead Purple'

Mature Height: 8" – 12"

USDA Plant Hardiness Zones: 7 – 9

Light Requirements: Full sun preferred

Bloom Time: June – frost

'Homestead Purple' Verbena blooms from June through frost and spreads quickly to become 24" to 36" in diameter. It is an easy-care plant that makes a beautiful edging for the butterfly garden. It produces a nectar that is irresistible to Swallowtails.

Verbena 'Homestead Purple' is a tough, heat- and drought-tolerant perennial. Only rarely is it bothered by insect pests or disease. It's only drawback may be that it is only hardy to zone 7. If you live north of zone 7, you have to treat it as an annual (as I do here in Pennsylvania). But because it does such a great job of luring those beautiful Swallowtails, it may be worth having even if you must purchase new plants every spring.

Stonecrop 'Autumn Joy'

Sedum spectabile 'Autumn Joy'

Mature Height: 30" – 36"

USDA Plant Hardiness Zones: 3 – 8

Light Requirements: Full sun or part shade

Bloom Time: July – September

Easy to grow, 'Autumn Joy' Stonecrop is a drought-tolerant perennial with thick, succulent leaves. Its star-shaped flowers are borne in domed clusters in late summer. The flowers are mauve-pink, turning deep pink as they mature.

'Autumn Joy' was among the plants I incorporated into my first butterfly garden in 1993. That summer, several butterfly species nectared heavily on the blossoms. In later years, though, it was rarely visited by butterflies. I began to think of this plant as a low-rate butterfly attractant.

Then Andy (my husband) and I visited Lancaster County in the fall of 2011, and there we were overwhelmed by the number of butterflies we saw on the 'Autumn Joy' Sedums that were then in full bloom. On some of the larger clumps, there were literally dozens of Fritillaries, Sulphurs, Buckeyes, and Cabbage Whites.

Lilac

Syringa vulgaris

Mature Height: 8' – 18'

USDA Plant Hardiness Zones: 3 – 8

Light Required: Full sun preferred

Bloom Time: May

There are dozens of Lilac species and hundreds of named varieties to choose from. Most are highly fragrant and grow 8' to 18' high. Flower color may be white, lavender, pink, blue, or deep purple.

Lilacs are long-lived, durable shrubs that prefer slightly alkaline soil. When a specimen grows too tall, it can be heavily pruned, with pruning being done shortly after blooming has finished.

While Lilacs bloom too early to be enjoyed by most butterfly species, they are popular with Swallowtails and other nectar-seekers that abound in May. In recent years, new dwarf cultivars have been introduced into the market, with some of these blooming weeks after the old-fashioned, Common Lilac has finished. 'Miss Kim' (*Syringa patula* 'Miss Kim'), is one of the newer, later-blooming cultivars. It is hardy, fragrant, and matures at just 5' high.

Artemisia 'Silver Brocade'

Artemisia stelleriana 'Silver Brocade'

Mature Height: 8" – 12"

USDA Plant Hardiness Zones: 6 – 9

Light Requirements: Full sun or part shade

Bloom Time: Late June thru July

'Silver Brocade' Artemisia is a low-growing, fast-spreading perennial. It actually does bloom but most people don't notice its flowers because they blend right into the beautiful silver-gray foliage (which looks and feels somewhat like velvet or felt).

I highly recommend Artemisia 'Silver Brocade' for the butterfly garden because it attracts both American Lady and Painted Lady butterflies for egg-laying. Years ago, I discovered American Lady caterpillars on the plants I was growing at the nursery. The next year, I put several of these plants into the butterfly garden. Since then, we have found American Lady and/or Painted Lady caterpillars on our 'Silver Brocade' every summer. Even when *"the Ladies"* have availability to thistle, Hollyhock, Balsam, Borage, and Pearly Everlasting (their well known hosts), they usually choose to lay their eggs on the 'Silver Brocade'.

Artemisia 'Silver Brocade' makes a great plant for the front edge of the butterfly garden. Alternate this plant with Verbena 'Homestead Purple' and you will have a beautiful edging for the butterfly garden. Set the plants into the garden at 30" to 36" apart though, because both of these are rapid spreaders.

Rue (also known as Herb-of-Grace)

Ruta graveolens

Mature Height: 24" – 36"

Light Requirements: Full or part sun.

USDA Zone Hardiness: 5– 9

Bloom Time: July thru August

Rue, also known as Herb-of-Grace, is native to southeastern Europe and is generally grown for its attractive bluish-green foliage. Some people plant it because they say it deters both dogs and cats from coming around.

I don't really know if there is any truth to Rue being able to dissuade dogs and cats from visiting. In the butterfly garden, though, it is a nursery for Black Swallowtail and Giant Swallowtail butterflies, since their caterpillars are able to feed on it. Rue produces clusters of tiny yellow flowers in mid-summer and it is both heat- and drought-tolerant.

Rue should be handled with care as some people are allergic to it. For some, Rue produces burn-like blisters on the skin. Because of this, you might consider planting Rue where it can be seen but seldom touched, at least until you are sure you are not allergic to it.

Some plants didn't make my Top 20 list but do deserve honorable mention. These include (in no particular order):

~ New England Aster *(Aster novae-angliae)*

~ Gloriosa Daisy *(Rudbeckia hirta)*

~ Blanket Flower *(Gaillardia grandiflora)*

~ Stokes Aster *(Stokesia laevis)*

~ Goldenrod *(Solidago)*

~ Lavender *(Lavandula)*

~ Sweet William *(Dianthus barbatus)*

~ Anise Hyssop *(Agastache 'Blue Fortune')*

~ Catmint *(Nepeta x faassenii)*

~ Oxeye *(Heliopsis helianthoides)*

~ Garden Phlox (cultivars other than 'Jeana')

~ Sage *(Salvia memorosa)*

Keep in mind that with just a few exceptions, most of the plants I have featured in this part of the book are nectar plants. As you learned though, host plants are of vital importance, and, as you can, you should incorporate host plants in or near your butterfly garden. Hops *(Humulus lupulus)* is a vine I would highly recommend. It attracts several butterflies for egg-laying (see page 23) and is easy to grow.

The Search Continues......

Can I say that my list of the-best-of-the-best butterfly-attracting plants won't change a little in the years to come? Of course not. For as long as I am able to garden, I will likely be experimenting with new plants in my butterfly garden.

Every year new plants will be introduced into the market and some of them will likely prove to be excellent butterfly lures.

And there are still a few flowering plants alleged to be irresisitable to butterflies which I have not yet tested in my gardens. Among these are mountain mint and Buttonbush. It could be that once I have rated and ranked these, my best-of-the-best list will be changed and re-arranged.

Hops (above)

A Comma laying an egg on Hops (left)

Author's Note: Most of my proofreaders suggested that I italicize the words Scabiosa, Verbena, Cosmos, Zinnia, Artemisia, and others, everywhere they were used in the book. Because I often use these words as commom names, rather than scientific genera, I opted to not italicize where I was employing the words as common names. Likely, my choice was grammatically incorrect. I apologize to my proofreaders and everyone in my audience who consider my nonitalicized genus names to be of incorrect English grammar.

A Clouded Sulphur, a Buckeye, and two Meadow Fritillaries enjoying the nectar of Sedum 'Autumn Joy' in Lancaster County, PA.

Part V

The Butterflies You Might See In Your Garden

Part V: The Butterflies You Might See In Your Garden

The Dances of Butterflies

In a popular song released in 1966, Bob Lind sang, "I chase the bright elusive butterfly of love." Some butterflies do seem elusive and sneaky, darting past you like a streak of lightning and then disappearing into the shadow of a tree. Others appear relaxed and neighborly, fluttering slowly and steadily over the meadows and pathways where you walk. Some butterflies tend to bounce and skip through the air while others glide and sail like eagles on open wings.

I think of Swallowtails and Monarchs as little ballerinas. With elegance, poise, and grace they seemingly dance their way from garden to garden, then softly tiptoe from flower to flower. Sometimes I can almost hear soft classical music playing in the background as I watch these butterflies move. Some butterflies are not elegant and graceful but, rather, appear to be nervous or hurried. Their flight more resembles a dance like the jitterbug, rumba, or jive.

Once you begin noticing butterflies, you begin to note characteristics and patterns that are unique to certain butterfly species. Painted Ladies, American Ladies, and Red Admirals are difficult to keep in sight because their flight is strong, fast, and zigzagging. Baltimore Checkerspots and Pearl Crescents are easy to follow because their flight is slow and generally they fly just above the growing vegetation.

Monarchs and Viceroys look almost identical but by watching them in flight you can generally distinguish between the two. Monarchs typically glide with their wings in a "V" whereas Viceroys glide on flat, horizontal wings.

Paying close attention to butterflies on warm summer mornings, you become aware that the different butterfly species appear every day in the same orderly procession. Cabbage Whites are generally the first butterflies to appear in the garden, followed by Sulphurs, Fritillaries, Swallowtails, and then Monarchs. Apparently the temperature at which butterflies are able to fly is different among the different species. But humidity somehow plays a role in the equation too, for on warm, humid mornings, Monarchs are often the first butterflies to appear in the garden.

Butterflies don't all behave the same. Some are social animals while others are territorial. Some always stay near the ground whereas others fly high into the sky. Most feed solely on flower nectar, others rarely visit flowers. Some love the sweet juice found in fruit but others seek out dung and carrion when hungry.

The Romantic Dance of Two Giant Swallowtails

The most romantic dance I have ever witnessed among butterflies was one involving a male and female Giant Swallowtail. And not only was I fortunate enough to see it, but my husband saw it too.

Actually, it was Andy who first noticed that a Giant Swallowtail was following another one everywhere it went. While the one butterfly, a female, nectared on Butterfly Bush, the other, a male, hovered in midair just inches above her. When the female left one Butterfly Bush to go nectar on another, the male fluttered closely behind.

For twenty minutes, we watched in awe as this pair of Swallowtails floated through our yard from one location to another. Flying with slow wingbeats and periodic glides, they rather resembled two miniature yellow and black-winged angels as they drifted by.

A pair of Giant Swallowtails in the garden.

Then off to the top of a tall tree the pair flew. They didn't stay there long though, only about a half hour.

For the remainder of the afternoon, the two Swallowtails alternated between gliding through our yard and resting in the tall trees in the woods. Not once did we see the male nectaring though. He seemed interested in nothing other than protecting the female from the dangers of the world.

At one point, the female interrupted her nectaring to hover over a patch of Rue. We wondered if she might be assuring this male of her cunning wisdom—in knowing exactly where to deposit her eggs, eggs which might this evening be fertilized by him.

To Andy and me, it appeared this couple was in love. I could almost hear Elvis Presley's *Love Me Tender* playing in the background.

Around 6:00 PM, the two Giant Swallowtails retreated to the woods and we never saw the pair together again. The next day, though, I spotted a female laying eggs on the Rue and wondered if this might be the same female we had watched the day before.

Choosing The Featured Butterflies

In choosing the butterflies that would be featured in this book, I first and foremost chose those which I have encountered in my own gardens, for these are the butterflies that I have come to know. In narrowing down the list, I chose those that are common and abundant in at least the eastern half of the nation. Finally, I strived to include some that are regularly seen throughout all or most of the contiguous 48 states. The butterflies that are likely to be seen in any garden in the U.S. include the Tiger Swallowtail, Cabbage White, Clouded Sulphur, Gray Hairstreak, Buckeye, Mourning Cloak, Painted Lady, Red Admiral, and Monarch.

Hundreds of butterfly species are native to the U.S. In even the busiest of butterfly gardens, though, only thirty or so species might be seen in any given summer. Many of these are illustrated on the pages that follow.

This book is not a field guide. Its intent is only to get you started on a fast track to butterfly gardening. If your interest deepens and you wish to identify every butterfly you encounter in your garden, in the mountains, on the desert, or in boggy wetlands, I suggest you purchase a field guide that encompasses the butterflies of the region you are exploring.

I have chosen to illustrate the featured butterflies according to their size. The largest butterflies, those in the Swallowtail family, are presented first; the smallest ones, shown last.

For each of the butterflies illustrated, both its common name and scientific name are shown. Also presented for each species are the plants most often utilized as caterpillar hosts, as well as the life stage in which it over-winters. In the description is information pertaining to the range in which the butterfly is found, the months it is most likely to be seen, and the flowers it most often nectars on in my garden.

Toward the bottom of many pages, I present blocks of information which did not manage to get incorporated elsewhere in the book. After assimilating some of these tidbits, you will likely realize that not everything you were taught in the past about butterflies is true. Some things are nothing more than myth.

In the order in which they appear (largest to smallest), these butterflies are presented on the pages that follow:

1. Giant Swallowtail
2. Tiger Swallowtail
3. Spicebush Swallowtail
4. Black Swallowtail
5. Monarch
6. Red-Spotted Purple
7. White Admiral
8. Mourning Cloak
9. Viceroy
10. Aphrodite Fritillary
11. Variegated Fritillary
12. Painted Lady
13. Red Admiral
14. Hackberry Emperor
15. Clouded Sulphur
16. Question Mark
17. Buckeye
18. Milbert's Tortoiseshell
19. Baltimore Checkerspot
20. Meadow Fritillary
21. Cabbage White
22. Gray Hairstreak
23. Pearl Crescent
24. Eastern Tailed Blue

The White Admiral will be shown alongside the Red-Spotted Purple because it is actually the same species as the Red-Spotted Purple. On some pages, where space allowed, I picture butterflies that are similar (and related) to the butterfly featured on that page, and in most instances, explain how you can distinguish one from the other.

Giant Swallowtail

Papilio cresphontes

Wingspan: 4" – 6"

Host plants: Prickly Ash, Rue, Gas Plant, Citrus

Broods per year: 2

Overwinter as: Pupae

Photo © Edith Smith

Giant Swallowtails are the largest of all the North American Swallowtails. They have dark brown (almost black) wings with bold yellow bands. The most prominent one runs from the outermost tip of its forewing toward its thorax. This yellow band is usually wider on the male. Looking at a Giant Swallowtail with closed wings, its underside is mostly cream with bands of black, a wide band of blue, and a few small orange spots. Its body is also cream in color.

The Giant Swallowtail's range includes Indiana, Illinois, Ohio, Pennsylvania, and all states south of there, then west to the Rocky Mountains. They are most abundant July through September. Their favorite garden flowers include Butterfly Bush, Zinnia, Phlox 'Jeana', and Verbena 'Homestead Purple'. Males participate in puddling. They generally flutter their wings while feeding, making it difficult to capture their vivid beauty in photos.

In our yard, we see just a few Giant Swallowtails each summer. A few years ago, I watched a female deposit eggs on one of our Gas Plants *(Dictamnus)* in mid August. The eggs hatched, and to my surprise, the caterpillars fed contently on the plant. I was astounded by this because I had never seen Gas Plant listed as a host for Giant Swallowtails. When the caterpillars were about ten days old and looking very healthy, my husband and I left home for a week-long vacation. While we were gone, our area was hit by two heavy frosts and the caterpillars were killed.

Aside from utilizing Gas Plant as a host in our yard, they also regularly deposit their eggs on Rue. In Florida, they lay their eggs on Citrus trees or Rue. The caterpillars resemble bird droppings.

Giant Swallowtail laying an egg.

Caterpillar: from a distance; and a closeup of its face.

Caterpillar attached to a stem, ready to pupate.

Giant Swallowtail chrysalis.

A male Tiger Swallowtail.

Tiger Swallowtail

Papilio glaucus

Wingspan: 3 1/2" – 5"

Host plants: Black Cherry, Tulip Tree, and Aspen

Broods per year: 2 – 3

Overwinter as: Pupae

A female Tiger Swallowtail.

Tiger Swallowtails generally fly with slow wingbeats. While nectaring, they are among the easiest of butterflies to approach. If they are disturbed though (say by someone getting too close to snap a photo), they quickly fly away, often high to the tops of trees.

Most Tiger Swallowtails have wings that are bright yellow with black stripes. A small percentage of the females lack the yellow stripes and appear to be just black. Look closely, though, and you can usually see a shadow-like trace of the tiger pattern. Females (both forms) have a patch of iridescent blue toward the bottom of their hindwings. This makes males and females easy to distinguish from one another.

Tiger Swallowtails are common in most of the contiguous 48 states, but those in the western states are known as Western Tiger Swallowtails *(Papillio rutulus)* and are said to be of a different population.

Tiger Swallowtails are among the first of butterflies to be seen in spring, and are often spotted nectaring on Lilacs. They are most abundant in May, and then again, July through August. They tend to fly higher than most other Swallowtails.

After the Lilacs have finished blooming, their favorite nectar sources include Butterfly Bush, Purple Coneflower, Common Milkweed, Swamp Milkweed, and Phlox 'Jeana'. The males engage in puddling.

Most Tiger Swallowtails are bright yellow. Ocassionally though, a dark form female, like the one pictured right, will appear in the garden for nectar.

Spicebush Swallowtail

Papilio troilus

Wingspan: 3 1/2" – 4 1/8"

Host plants: Spicebush, Sassafras

Broods per year: 2

Overwinter as: Pupae

A male Spicebush Swallowtail.

Like several other Swallowtails, the Spicebush Swallowtail is predominately black. Looking down onto its open wings, there is a single row of creamy white spots along the outer edge of the forewing and hindwing. On the lower portion of the hindwing, a male has a large patch of bluish gray-green whereas the female has a patch of iridescent blue.

Spicebush Swallowtails generally reside in wooded areas and the fields adjacent to the woods. In native wooded habitats, they nectar on plants such as Jewelweed, Joe-Pye Weed, and Honeysuckle. In residential gardens, they often nectar on Butterfly Bush, Phlox 'Jeana', Zinnia, and Verbena 'Homestead Purple'.

By knowing that Spicebush Swallowtails tend to reside near wooded areas, you can generally conclude that if you see a black-colored Swallowtail in an urban area where there are no forests nearby, it is not likely a Spicebush Swallowtail.

Spicebush Swallowtails are most abundant July through August, but may be spotted anytime from April through September. They tend to fly a bit lower than other Swallowtails and they fly with rapid, directional flight. While nectaring, they flutter their wings.

We have planted several Spicebushes in our yard so that we can periodically look for Spicebush caterpillars. One of our favorite caterpillars, they begin life looking like a bird dropping (pictured below, left), and then become bright green with huge eyespots resembling snake eyes (pictured below, center). Usually, just a day or two before they pupate, the caterpillars turn bright orange (like the one shown below, right). You might find a caterpillar inside the rolled, taco-style leaf of a Spicebush (unless it has already left that leaf for another).

Spicebush Swallowtails might be seen in any state that lies east of the Mississippi River.

Black Swallowtail

Papilio polyxenes

Wingspan: 3 1/8" – 4"

Host plants: **Parsley, Dill, Fennel, Rue**

Broods per year: **2 – 3**

Overwinter as: **Pupae**

A male Black Swallowtail.

A female Black Swallowtail.

The Black Swallowtail is one of several Swallowtails that are predominantly black. But the Black Swallowtail can easily be distinguished from the other black ones by a single yellow spot on its upper forewing. The arrows in the photos on this page point to that identifying yellow mark.

The male has a bright yellow, wide median band on its wings. The female is distinguished from him by the bold patch of blue on her lower hindwing.

The Black Swallowtail's distribution range includes all of the states that lie east of the Rocky Mountains, and into Arizona, too. They like open areas like fields, meadows, and gardens created for butterflies.

Black Swallowtails are commonly seen from May through September but are most abundant in July and August. They generally fly lower than most Swallowtails and their flight often appears to be non-directional.

Black Swallowtail males engage in hilltopping, a behavior which involves flying over small hills in search of females. They are sometimes territorial too, chasing other males from their hilltops. Males also engage in puddling.

Among the Black Swallowtail's favorite nectar sources are Lilac, Butterfly Bush, Cosmos, Zinnia, Phlox 'Jeana', and Milkweed. When they feed, their wings flutter constantly, making it difficult to get a crisp photo of them.

In undisturbed areas of North America, they lay their eggs on Queen Anne's Lace, but the caterpillars are also able to feed on Parsley, Dill, Fennel, and Rue. And where these plants are offered, the females will readily lay their eggs on them.

Left: A Black Swallowtail caterpillar feeding on Rue.

Right: Notice that the yellow dot which identifies this butterfly as a Black Swallowtail is evident on its underside too.

The Butterflies You Might See In Your Garden

Monarch

Danaus plexippus

Wingspan: 3 1/2" – 4 1/4"

Host plants: Milkweed

Broods per year: 3 - 5

Overwinter as: Adults

A female Monarch

A male. The white arrows point to the black ovals that identify this Monarch as a male.

The Monarch is the most well known butterfly in North America. It is the largest orange and black butterfly in the U.S., but that is not the reason for its fame. The Monarch's popularity comes from its annual, bird-like, north and south migration to and from Mexico.

After mating in Mexico in late February, Monarchs begin their northward journey. They (actually the offspring of those that overwintered in Mexico) reach the northern range of their distribution (which extends into Canada) sometime in June. There Monarchs reside and multiply all summer and then, in late August, begin the migration southward again. In the central mountains of Mexico, in the Oyamel fir forests, Monarchs overwinter in a relatively inactive state.

A male Monarch has a conspicuous oval-shaped scent patch on each of his hindwings, making it easy to distinguish from a female. Monarchs flap and glide when they fly. When they are gliding, their wings are usually in a "V".

Among the Monarch's favorite nectar sources are Butterfly Bush, Purple Coneflower, Milkweed, Rocky Mountain Blazing Star, Zinnia, Brazilian Verbena, and Mexican Sunflower.

Female Monarchs lay their eggs on Milkweed *(Asclepias)*, the caterpillars' host plant. As the caterpillars consume Milkweed foliage, they also consume cardiac glycosides which are produced by the plant. The cardiac glycosides are absorbed by the caterpillar and remain in the body of the insect throughout its lifespan. Cardiac glycosides are distasteful and toxic to birds, causing them to become extremely ill. Whether a bird consumes a Monarch caterpillar or an adult butterfly, it will likely become ill, vomit, and vow to never eat another Monarch.

Not all Monarchs migrate to Mexico. It is generally believed that those residing east of the Rocky Mountains migrate to Mexico, while those residing west of the Rocky Mountains migrate to the coast of California for the winter. In California, the largest overwintering sites are located along the central coast, from Santa Cruz to Los Angles counties. Monarchs fly year around in Florida and, thus, do not migrate. During the summer, Monarchs might be seen in any of the 48 contiguous states.

One Species.........

Red-Spotted Purple

Limenitis arthemis astyanax

Wingspan: 3 1/8" – 4 1/8"

Host plants: Wild Cherry, Aspen, Poplar, or Willow

Broods per year: 2

Overwinter as: Larvae

One Species, Two Different Forms.....Once believed to be two different species, it is now widely accepted that the Red-Spotted Purple and the White Admiral are actually of the same species.

The range of the Red-Spotted Purple includes New Jersey, Pennsylvania, Ohio, Indiana, Illinois, Iowa and the states to the south of that, and then east to the Mississippi River. The range of the White Admiral includes New Jersey, Pennsylvania, Ohio, Michigan, Wisconsin, Minnesota and points north (extending into most of Canada and even up through the center of Alaska).

In the states where both Red-Spotted Purples and White Admirals are found (notably New Jersey, Pennsylvania, New York, and Massachusetts), these two very different looking butterflies mate to produce offspring. For them to mate, they must be of the same species. In the area where the Red-Spotted Purples and the White Admirals mate, the offspring may carry traits of each parent, confusing people who are trying to determine what species they actually are.

Here in the center of Pennsylvania, Red-Spotted Purples are plentiful while White Admirals are quite rare, a sight to behold.

The Red-Spotted Purple is blue-black with iridescent blue toward the bottom of its hindwings. It also has orange spots along the outer edges of the forewing.

Its underwings are mostly blue-black with a band of blue along the outer edge of both its forewing and hindwing. Numerous bright orange spots also adorn the underwing.

A Red-Spotted Purple feasting on overripe fruit: bananas, apples, and peaches.

........Two Different Forms

White Admiral

Limenitis arthemis arthemis

Wingspan: 3 1/8" – 4 1/8"

Host plants: Birch, Poplar, Aspen or Apple

Broods per year: 2

Overwinter as: Larvae

The White Admiral is mostly blue-black with a wide white band running the length of the forewing and hingwing. Blue spots also adorn the edges of both the forewing and hindwing. On the underside of the wings, the wide white band is prevalent as are lots of orange spots against the dull blue-black background.

Being of the same species, Red-spotted Purples and White Admirals are fond of Butterfly Bush, Common Milkweed, and Swamp Milkweed. Both participate in puddling; and both also dine on overripe fruit, dung, and carrion.

This species seems to prefer residing near moist woodlands but it is often seen in suburban areas also. They generally flap and glide while flying.

Both Red-Spotted Purples and White Admirals might be seen anytime between mid May and late September. They are most abundant June through August.

Northern gardeners might think that the Monarch is the only North American butterfly to lay its eggs on Milkweed. Not true. The Queen (Danaus gilippus) which resides in Florida, Texas, and Arizona year around, also utilizes Milkweed as its host.

In summer, Queens migrate northward, especially up through the center of the U.S., and are often spotted as far north as Wyoming, Nebraska, and Iowa.

On its upperside, the Queen is an orangish chestnut-brown. The outer edges of its wings are edged in black, while two rows of white spots are evident on the forewing. Looking at a Queen's underside, it closely resembles a Monarch (and the Monarch is closely related to the Queen).

Queens lay their eggs singly on Milkweed and their caterpillars look similar to those of the Monarch. Note that a Queen larva has three pair of long black filaments whereas a Monarch caterpillar has two (see photo to left). Its chrysalis, too, closely resembles the Monarch's.

Queens inhabit open, sunny areas such as fields, deserts, pastures, gardens, and waterways. They are about the same size as Monarchs.

Mourning Cloak

Nymphalis antiopa

Wingspan: 2 5/8" – 4"

Host plants: **Willow, Elm, Birch, Hackberry, Poplar**

Broods per year: 1 - 2

Overwinter as: Adults

Mourning Cloaks are large butterflies that are easy to identify. They are dark brown (almost black) with a creamy yellow border running along the outer edge of each wing. Just inside the yellow border are numerous blue spots. On the underside of its folded wings, the creamy yellow border is prominent while the remainder of the wings are dark in color. When they fly by, sometimes gliding rather than flapping, you won't likely see the blue spots—but you will know by the unmistakable yellow border that you have seen a Mourning Cloak.

Mourning Cloaks are widespread, residing in all of the 48 contiguous states. They are common in wooded areas, fields, along roadsides, and in downtown urban areas.

Mourning Cloaks overwinter as adults, finding protection wherever they can. On warm spring days they sometimes exit their dormant state for a brief period in search of tree sap. Aside from tree sap, this butterfly likes to feast on fruit. Occasionally they have been spotted nectaring on Common Milkweed. Males engage in puddling. Northern gardeners might lure them into their yards by offering rotting fruit in April and May.

A female Mourning Cloak laying eggs on Willow.

Female Mourning Cloaks lay their eggs in clusters, generally on Willow trees. When the caterpillars hatch, they feed communally, sometimes lining up side by side with their heads all facing toward the outside of a leaf.

Male Mourning Cloaks are territorial, chasing intruding males away. Most often their territory consists of about 300 square yards.

Entomologists believe this may be our longest living butterfly, with adults living ten to eleven months.

The Saddleback caterpillar (shown on the next page) is not the only stinging caterpillar. Others include the Hag Moth caterpillar, Hackberry Leaf Slug, Flannel moth caterpillar, Io Moth caterpillar, and the Puss caterpillar. All of these larvae mature to become moths, not butterflies.

Three of the above mentioned caterpillars utilize Hackberry as a host plant. These are the Io Moth caterpillar, the Puss caterpillar, and the Hackberry Leaf Slug. Before touching any caterpillar you find on Hackberry trees, be sure it is a butterfly caterpillar and not one of the stinging moth caterpillars.

If you develop an interest in caterpillars, consider purchasing a field guide that encompasses the caterpillars of the area you are exploring. With that in hand, you should be able to identify most of the caterpillars you find.

And remember that 99.9% of the caterpillars you encounter will be harmless . They can do nothing more than tickle your hand with their feet as they crawl across it.

Viceroy

Limenitis archippus

Wingspan: 2 1/2" – 3 1/4"

Host plants: Willow

Broods per year: 2 - 3

Overwinter as: Larvae

The Viceroy looks a lot like a Monarch with one notable difference. The Viceroy has a vivid black line running across its hindwing, whereas the Monarch does not. With wings closed, this black line is prominent on the underside too. Viceroys are generally smaller than Monarchs. Like Monarchs, the Viceroy flaps and glides while flying; but while gliding, the Viceroy's wings are usually flat (horizontal) whereas the Monarch glides with its wings in a "V".

Viceroys are most commonly found where Willows grow, especially if a stream or wetland lies close by. They might be seen in any of the contiguous 48 states and are commonly observed between June and September.

Viceroy larvae (caterpillars) and pupae (chrysalises) both resemble bird droppings, making them inconspicuous to predators. And since the adult Viceroy mimics the toxic, distasteful Monarch, they are rarely the victims of bird attacks.

In my garden, Viceroys rarely nectar on anything other than Butterfly Bush. They also feed on tree sap, rotting fruit, and dung. Males participate in puddling.

Stinging Caterpillars

Sketch by Rob Franklin

Look at, but do not touch, this caterpillar.
The Saddleback caterpillar is the larva of a brown stout-bodied moth that is native to the eastern U.S. The slug-like caterpillar, which is about 1" long at maturity, is brown at its head and rear, and predominately pea-green in the center. Near the center of its back, it sports a brown spot edged in white. Looking at the caterpillar, it actually appears to have a saddle on its back and, hence, its name.
The foliage of many plants, shrubs, and trees are utilized as hosts for the Saddleback caterpillar. Among them are apple, ash, birch, maple, oak, sassafras, cherry, plum, elm, dogwood, spirea, rose, sunflower, and corn.
The caterpillar has a pair of fleshy "horns" near its front and rear. These horns, and the many hairs that cover the caterpillar's body, secrete a venomous sting when touched. The sting, which is quite painful, can cause swelling, nausea, a high fever, and/or a rash that can last for days. Do not touch this caterpillar!

Aphrodite Fritillary

Speyeria aphrodite

Wingspan: 2 1/2" – 3 1/4"

Host plants: Violets

Broods per year: 1

Overwinter as: Larvae

Aphrodite Fritillaries are smaller than most of the large butterflies but larger than most of the medium-sized ones. They fly rapidly and continuously flap their wings. When they are nectaring on flowers, they can usually be approached quite easily.

Aphrodite Fritillaries are brownish-orange, mottled with spots and patches of black. On the underside of their hindwing, a narrow sub-marginal cream-colored band is evident, as are many showy silvery-white spots. The forewing is mostly dull orange with splotches of black.

There are several Fritillary species that closely resemble the Aphrodite Fritillary in both color and size, one of them being the Great Spangled Fritillary. Without a field guide, it is difficult to distinguish between them.

The Aphrodite Fritillary resides mostly in the upper two thirds of the contiguous U.S. It is commonly found in fields and meadows, along roadsides, and other open areas. In the wild, they are often found nectaring on Milkweed, Mint, and Thistle. In cultivated gardens, they are fond of Butterfly Bush, Milkweed, Purple Coneflower, Zinnia, Rocky Mountain Blazing Star, Coreopsis, Sedum, and Cosmos.

Aphrodite Fritillaries have a unique life cycle which revolves around the life cycle of violets. The eggs hatch in the fall and the tiny caterpillars immediately hibernate for the winter, finding refuge in the soil. The next spring, when violets are growing vigorously, the caterpillars exit dormancy and begin to feed on them. Once the caterpillars are full grown, they pupate. Adults begin to emerge from chrysalises around mid-June and continue to emerge for the next month or so. By autumn, only gravid females remain alive. Females deposit eggs from summer through fall (where violets will grow in spring) and the cycle begins again.

This Great Spangled Fritillary is difficult to distinguish from an Aphrodite Fritillary.

Variegated Fritillary

Euptoieta claudia

Wingspan: 2" – 3"

Host plants: Violets, Passion Vine

Broods per year: 3 - 4

Overwinter as: Adult (in the south only)

Variegated Fritillaries are medium-sized butterflies with wing edges that are somewhat scalloped. They generally fly low with shallow wing beats. When they are nectaring on flowers, they can sometimes be approached quite closely.

Variegated Fritillaries are dull, orange-brown, mottled with spots and wavy black lines. On the underside of their hindwing, a sub-marginal cream-colored band is prominent. They do not, however, have the silvery spots evident on the underside of most other Fritillaries.

The Variegated Fritillary is a permanent resident of the southern portions of the U.S. and migrates to northern states during the summer. With the exception of the Pacific Northwest, this butterfly might be spotted in any state within the contiguous U.S. and is commonly found in fields and meadows, along roadsides, and in other open areas. In the wild, they are often found nectaring on Milkweed, Mint, and Thistle. In cultivated gardens, they are fond of Butterfly Bush, Milkweed, Purple Coneflower, Zinnia, Coreopsis, Sedum, and Cosmos.

In the southern-most states, it usually utilizes Passion Vine as a host plant.

On page 13, I stated that miraculous changes take place inside a chrysalis. I'd like to elaborate on that.

Within days of pupating, the caterpillar actually begins to liquify inside the chrysalis as its tissues are systematically broken down. Part of its body, the prolegs for instance, are totally digested and all trace of them disappears. Other parts, the stomach for instance, are completely reconstructed, being reduced to one quarter the size it was in the full grown caterpillar. The simple eyes are replaced by complex eyes. The mouth is entirely changed in both form and function, from being a device used for cutting and chewing to being an apparatus that functions as a retractable drinking straw. Four wings emerge from the thorax and reproductive organs materialize inside the abdomen. And all of this occurs inside many chrysalises in less than two weeks. Miraculous? Yeah! This has to be one of the most phenomenal transformations to take place in nature.

Inside the chrysalis, the butterfly's proboscis actually develops as two long, separate pieces. Immediately upon eclosing (emerging from the chrysalis), the butterfly must assemble the two pieces into a single unit. Unless the two halves fit tightly together, liquids cannot be sucked through it, and the butterfly will die of starvation.

Painted Lady

Vanessa cardui

Wingspan: 2" – 2 7/8"

Host plants: Thistle, Hollyhock, Mallow, Balsam, and many more

Broods per year: 1 - 3

Overwinter as: Adult

The Painted Lady is the most widely distributed butterfly in the world. Here in the U.S., they reside year around in the southern-most states, then migrate northward to populate the northern states in spring and summer. In northern states, Painted Ladies are abundant in some years and scarce in others. When autumn arrives, they do not migrate south but, instead, stay put, freeze, and die. Then, the next summer, new migrants arrive from the South.

The upperside of a Painted Lady's wings are deep orange (sometimes with a pinkish cast) and black, with some white spots and splotches on the upper, outer edges of the forewings.

Underneath, their hindwing has numerous eye-spots. A "cobweb-like" effect covers the hindwing also. Toward the lower portion of the forewing, there is a visible patch of orangish-pink.

The summer range of the Painted Lady extends across the entire U.S. They are commonly seen in fields and meadows, along roadsides, and even near coastal dunes. They are regular visitors to the butterfly garden and often nectar on Butterfly Bush, Coreopsis, Milkweeds, and Joe-Pye Weed.

A close relative of the Painted Lady, the American Lady looks much like a Painted Lady, just a little smaller. They also reside in the South year around and then migrate northward in spring and summer. The American Lady has just two large eye-spots on the underside of her hindwing. From above, they look rather similar except for a single white dot on the forewing of the American Lady (which distinguishes one from the other). In the photo of the American Lady, below, a black arrow points to the white dot which identifies it as an American Lady.

Both Painted Ladies and American Ladies will readily lay their eggs on Artemisia 'Silver Brocade' and, for this reason, I suggest this plant be planted in or near the butterfly garden. You will know you have Painted Lady or American Lady larvae feeding on the Artemisia when you see the edges of leaves tied together with webbing. Each caterpillar constructs one of these tent-like structures to protect itself from predators.

American Lady

Red Admiral

Vanessa atalanta

Wingspan: 2" – 2 3/4"

Host plants: Stinging Nettle, Pellitory

Broods per year: 2

Overwinter as: Adult

The Red Admiral is closely related to the Painted Lady, the American Lady, and the Buckeye (shown on page 67). Like its relatives, the Red Admiral resides year around in the southern-most states and then expands its range northward during spring and summer.

The Red Admiral is black-brown and has a bright orange-red band along the outer margin of its hindwing and up through the center of the forewing. The outermost edges of the forewing are dark with splotches of white. On the underside of the forewing, red, white, and blue colored patches are evident, while the hindwing appears dark and mottled.

During the summer months, the Red Admiral might be seen in any of the contiguous 48 states. They are frequent visitors to gardens and often nectar on Butterfly Bush, Milkweeds, Coreopsis, and Zinnia. They also feed on tree sap and fruit. Red Admirals are fond of salt and sometimes alight on the exposed skin of sweaty gardeners so that they might feed on the salt in perspiration.

When searching for mates, male Red Admirals are territorial. If another butterfly, a bird, or even a person enters the territory a male has claimed, he will generally leave his perch to investigate. Patrolling males have been known to chase other Red Admiral males, and even birds, out of their territory. When the intruder is gone, he returns to his perch to again watch for potential mates.

The Harvester butterfly (Feniseca tarquinius) is unique in many ways:

The adult butterfly has a very short proboscis and feeds only on the honeydew secreted by aphids. They never feed on nectar.

The Harvester caterpillars are the only North American species to be carnivorous, feeding on woolly aphids and occasionally, scale insects. The caterpillars are also unique in that they have only four larval instars, whereas most butterfy larvae have five.

On its upperside, a Harvester is predominately orange-brown with black markings. Underneath, it is variegated orange brown with a faint purplish cast. Splotches of cream adorn its upper forewing. Its wingspan is 1 1/8" to 1 3/8". Harvesters produce two broods per year and overwinter as pupae (chrysalises).

While humans only rarely encounter this butterfly, its territory encompasses swampy areas and woodlands. Its range includes most of the eastern half of the U.S.

Hackberry Emperor

Asterocampa celtis

Wingspan: 1 1/2" – 2 1/2"

Host plants: Hackberry

Broods per year: 1 - 2

Overwinter as: Larvae

Photo © Edith Smith

Photo © Edith Smith

On its upperside, a Hackberry Emperor is mostly orangish-brown. It has one prominent eyespot on its forewing and many smaller ones on its hindwing. It also has many white spots on its forwing and a few more on its hindwing.

Underneath, it is predominantly cream, gray, and brown. There are striking eyespots on both the forewing and hindwing.

Hackberry Emperors are not often seen far away from Hackberry Trees, its larval host plant. Only rarely do they nectar, preferring to obtain most of their nutrients from tree sap, rotting fruit, dung, and carrion. They have been known to alight on sweaty people to consume the salt from perspiration.

The range of the Hackberry Emperor includes most of the eastern half of the U.S. While they are most often found near natural meadows, open woods, and fields, they do sometimes visit gardens for nectar. They might be enticed to visit the garden if overripe fruit is offered nearby.

Hackberry Emperors are hard to follow when they are flying because they fly fast. They might be observed anytime between June and September but are most abundant June and July.

Photo © Edith Smith

The Tawny Emperor (Asterocampa clyton) is a close relative of the Hackberry Empeor. Like its relative, the Tawny Emperor usually gets its nourishment from tree sap, rotting fruit, dung, and carrion. Its distribution range includes most of the eastern U.S.

The Tawny Emperor utilizes Hackberry as its host , and generally lays its eggs on the older leaves of the tree. Eggs are laid in clusters of seventy-five or more.

Rarely does this butterfly stray far from the Hackberry tree. You might attract it by offering a plate of overripe fruit.

Clouded Sulphur

Colias philodice

Wingspan: 1 3/4" – 2 3/4"

Host plants: Clover, Alfafa, False Indigo

Broods per year: 3 – 4

Overwinter As: Larvae or Pupae

Sulphurs are medium-sized yellow butterflies. Most fly low and rapid, and tend to make very short stops when they nectar. When they are nectaring, their wings are closed, making it difficult to distinguish one Sulphur from another.

There are many different Sulphurs and most closely resemble one another. To name just a few, there is the Clouded Sulphur, the Cloudless Sulphur, the Pink-edged Sulphur, the Southern Dogface Sulphur, and the Orange Sulphur (which, as the name implies, is yellow with a patch of orange). The Clouded Sulphur is also known as the Common Sulphur, and the Orange Sulphur as the Alfalfa Sulphur. Adding to the difficulty in distinguishing between the different Sulphurs, the Orange Sulphur and the Clouded Sulphur often interbreed to create all sorts of variations.

Unless you have a field guide and a strong determination to distinguish one Sulphur from another, just do as I do and simply group them all together as "Sulphurs". With so many Sulphurs residing in the U.S., there are bound to be a few species in your area, no matter where you live. They are frequent visitors to butterfly gardens and often nectar on Butterfly Bush, Zinnia, Phlox 'Jeana', Mexican Sunflower, Purple Coneflower, and Sedum. They also engage in puddling.

Sulphurs might be observed anytime from mid-April through late October. They are most abundant, however, July through September.

Some Sulphurs will utilize False Indigo *(Baptisia australis)*, Wild Senna *(Cassia hebecarpa)*, or Ornamental Clover *(Trifolium rubens* 'Red Feathers') as host plants.

Sulphurs are difficult to distinguish from one another. Since the Sulphur pictured above left appears to have a patch of orange on its forewing, I presume it to be an Orange Sulphur (also known as an Alfalfa Sulphur). The other two are likely Clouded Sulphurs, though I wouldn't bet anything of importance on that.

Question Mark

Polygonia interrogationis

Wingspan: 2 1/8" – 2 7/8"

Host plants: Elm, Hackberry, Nettle

Broods per year: 2

Overwinter As: Adult

The Question Mark is predominately orange and black with jagged outer wings which are edged in gray-blue. On the underside, it has a silvery "?" mark, which is what gives the butterfly its name. Aside from the silver markings, the Question Mark's underside is camouflaged to blend almost perfectly into tree bark.

The Question Mark's flight is rapid and zigzagging, making it difficult to keep in sight. It is resident to most of the eastern two thirds of the U.S., and they are most abundant in woodlands and adjacent open areas.

Only rarely do these butterflies nectar, preferring instead to gather nutrients from tree sap, fruit, dung, and carrion. When I do see them nectaring, they are on either Butterfly Bush or Milkweed. Question Marks overwinter as adults and are generally among the first of butterfly species to appear in spring. Northern gardeners might try luring them into their yard with overripe fruit in April and May.

Question Mark eggs, closeup.

Question Mark caterpillar

Question Mark chrysalis

The Butterflies You Might See In Your Garden

Buckeye

Junonia coenia

Wingspan: 1 5/8" – 2 3/4"

Host plants: Plantain, Snapdragon, Verbena bonariensis

Broods per year: 2 - 3

Overwinter as: Adult

Buckeyes are predominately brown with six striking eye-spots along the outer margins of its wings. There is one large eyespot on each forewing, surrounded by a patch of cream. Also, on the forewing's upper edge are two vertical bright orange bars. Two eyespots adorn each of the hindwings.

The underside of the hindwing is mostly soft beige with small eyespots while the forewing is adorned by the large eye-spot which, too, is surrounded by cream. The two vertical orange bars also appear on the underside of the forewing.

Buckeyes are closely related to Painted Ladies, American Ladies, and Red Admirals. All four of these butterfly species inhabit the southern-most parts of the U.S. the year around. In spring, they begin to migrate northward to populate the northern states. They do not, however, make the return migration in fall. Instead, they simply freeze out in the northern states, only to be repopulated by new migrants the following year.

In summer, Buckeyes are common throughout most of the U.S. They tend to prefer open areas for nectaring and often nectar on Butterfly Bush, Coreopsis, Milkweed, and Sedum. They sometimes engage in puddling.

Male Buckeyes have a unique manner of seeking out mates. From morning through mid- afternoon they will sit on bare ground and patiently watch for other Buckeyes to fly overhead. When one does, he darts up to investigate. When the other Buckeye is a male, he soon returns to his perch. When the other butterfly is a female, he pursues her and, if she is receptive to his advances, they mate.

The Comma, which is also known as the Hop Merchant, is a close relative of the Question Mark and looks almost identical, but with one notable exception: the Comma has a silvery ",", branding on the underside of its hindwing whereas the Question Mark has the silver "?".

Commas are generally a bit smaller than Question Marks. Their tails are a bit shorter too. The Comma utilizes Hops, Nettle, and Elm as host plants.

Milbert's Tortoiseshell

Nymphalis milberti

Wingspan: 1 5/8" – 2 1/4"

Host plants: Nettle

Broods per year: 2

Overwinter as: Adults

A medium-sized butterfly, Milbert's Tortoiseshell is quite colorful. Its wings are dark brown to black with a wide band of yellow-orange running the length of their outermost edges. Two orange bars also adorn the upper edge of the forewing.

Underneath, its wings are mostly dark colored with a band of tan-brown near the outer edges. They are well camouflaged when perching on tree bark. Males often perch throughout the afternoon to watch for females.

The range of Milbert's Tortoiseshell includes the northern half of the contiguous states. Their favored habitats are moist pastures and fields that border woodlands with streams.

Milbert's Tortoiseshells frequently visit flower gardens for nectar. Among their favorite flowers are Butterfly Bush, Asters, and Milkweeds. They also feast on tree sap and fruit.

Skippers

On page 9, I stated that butterflies are divided into two superfamilies: the true butterflies and the skippers. True butterflies can generally be distinguished from skippers by being more colorful and having narrower bodies and longer antennae. All of the butterflies featured in Part V of this book are classified as true butterflies.

Most skippers are tawny-orange, brown, black, or gray. They are small- to medium-sized butterflies. Some, the folded-winged skippers, rest with their forewings and hindwings at different angles, somewhat resembling a folded paper airplane. A folded-wing skipper is pictured top left. Others, the spread-winged skippers, tend to perch with their wings open in the same plane, like the Wild Indigo Duskywing pictured bottom left.

Skippers have clubbed antennae and often the clubs are slightly hooked backward like a crochet hook. There are scores of skippers in the United States and most are difficult to distinguish from one another. Skippers are rapid, erratic flyers, seeming to skip from place to place, and hence, the reason for their name.

Baltimore Checkerspot

Euphydryas phaeton

Wingspan: 1 3/4" – 2 1/2"

Host plants: Turtlehead, Plantain, Penstemon

Broods per year: 1

Overwinter as: Larvae

Baltimore Checkerspots would not likely be mistaken for any other butterfly. They are mostly brown-black with orange and white spots. A band of orange spots runs along the outer margin of both the forewing and hindwing, while white spots dot the area just to the inside of this orange margin. Below, it is also brown-black, orange, and white, with these colors distributed in a dazzling pattern.

The Baltimore Checkerspot's range includes most of the eastern half of the U.S. Not included in its range are North Carolina, South Carolina, Georgia, Florida, Mississippi, and Louisiana. The Baltimore Checkerspot is very local in occurrence due to the spotty occurrence of Turtlehead, its host plant. Turtlehead usually grows near streams and wetlands.

Baltimores are easy to follow in flight as they fly slowly and usually just above the height of the surrounding vegetation. They are regular visitors to gardens and often nectar on Coreopsis, Zinnia, Cosmos, and Milkweed.

In providing host plants for Baltimore Checkerspots, I suggest you plant Turtlehead *(Chelone)* right next to Beardtongue *(Penstemon)*, with *Penstemon digitalis* 'Husker Red' being my recommendation. Female Baltimores will lay their eggs on Turtlehead, but then the next spring, when the caterpillars come out of their dormant state to continue their life cycle, they will most often feed on the Penstemon. The reason for this becomes obvious when you note that Turtlehead is often still dormant when the caterpillars emerge from their hibernation-like state in late spring. (See page 15 for Baltimore Checkerspot metamorphosis.)

In my opinion (and in that of many other butterfly enthusiasts also), Baltimore Checkerspots are losing ground in their fight to survive. In many states where they were common to abundant twenty years ago, they are now rarely seen. What a shame that this magnificent butterfly is disappearing from our sight.

Butterflies thru history:
In both Aztec and Mayan folklore, butterflies symbolized life and death. For the ancient Greeks, "psyche" was their word for "butterfly". Psyche literally meant "the soul."
In many civilations, it was believed that butterflies carry souls to Heaven.

Meadow Fritillary

Boloria bellona

Wingspan: 1 5/8" – 2"

Host plants: Violets

Broods per year: 1

Overwinter as: Larvae

The Meadow Fritiallary is dull orange-brown speckled with black splotches and spots. Looking at it from above, it appears darker toward its body (because there are larger splotches of black toward the body). The underside of its hindwing is mottled while the forewing is mostly dull orange-brown with black spots.

Meadow Fritillaries reside in most of the Northeast. They also reside in every state bordered by one of the Great Lakes. Meadow Fritillaries often choose to inhabit grassy fields and they are usually found flying close to the ground. Their flight might be characterized as slow and rather lazy.

Meadow Fritillaries often visit gardens for nectar. Among their favorite flowers are Gloriosa Daisy, Milkweed, and Sedum. They also acquire nutrients from dung.

The life cycle of the Meadow Fritillary is similar to that of the Great Spangled Fritillary, their close relative, as their host plant, too, is the violet.

Myth: If you hold a butterfly by its wings and rub off some of the powdery coating, the butterfly will die, or it will be unable to fly.
Fact: The powdery coating which rubs off the butterfly is actually the microscopic scales that were mentioned on page 9. In the course of a butterfly's daily living, some of these scales get rubbed off. A butterfly will not die, and it will not be unable to fly, if you gently hold it by its closed wings for just a few minutes.

Myth: Pupating butterfly larvae (caterpillars) spin a cocoon around themselves.
Fact: Pupating butterfly larvae do not spin a cocoon around themselves as many moths do. Instead, they simply shed their skin to become incased inside a chrysalis. The chrysalis is actually just another skin-like coating, but unlike the caterpillar's previous layers of skin, this one hardens to become a protective shell. Inside this protective shell, the caterpillar actually liquifies—and then solidifies again to become a butterfly.

Myth: Butterfly caterpillars are potentially destructive to trees, and in large numbers, can actually defoliate them.
Fact: The Gypsy Moth caterpillar, Eastern Tent caterpillar, Western Tent caterpillar, and Fall Webworm are among the culprits that can cause serious damage to trees. Each of these caterpillars matures to become a moth, not a butterfly. Butterfly larvae do not generally cause any serious damage to trees.

Cabbage White

Pieris rapae

Wingspan: 1 1/2" – 2"

Host plants: Cabbage, Broccoli, Nasturtium, Spider Flower *(Cleome)*

Broods per year: 3 - 5

Overwinter as: Pupae

The Cabbage White is not native to the U.S. They were accidentally introduced into Canada in 1860 and have since spread to extend their range to include all of the contiguous U.S. They are now the most common butterfly in the U.S.

Cabbage Whites are sometimes mistaken for moths. They are common to abundant in most states. Their habitats include urban areas, open fields, roadsides, and agricultural grounds. The larvae have been known to cause significant damage to cabbage, broccoli, brussels sprouts, and cauliflower crops.

Looking closely at the forewing of a Cabbage White, you will see either one or two black spots. If it has one spot, it is a male. Two spots identify it as a female.

Cabbage Whites engage in a behavior known as spiraling. When a female is not interested in mating and is approached by a male who is interested, she will fly in small circles high into the air. The male will chase her in circles until he finally gives up and drops to the ground. Fun to watch, this behavior is easily recognized.

In a butterfly garden, Cabbage Whites often nectar on Butterfly Bush, Brazilian Verbena, Nepeta, Zinnia, Sage, and Lavender. They generally feed with their wings closed.

I wanted to have a range map on every page in Part V, showing the territory in which each featured butterfly could be found. Unfortunately, there simply was not space for even a small map on many of the pages; so with that being the case, I opted to be consistent and omit maps completely.

In Part VI of the book, you will find a list of books and websites which do include range (distributon) maps. While I'm sure that most of these maps are pretty accurate, I recommend that you explore the maps on the Butterflies and Moths of North America website, www.butterfliesandmoths.org. Their maps are developed by registering the records of verified sightings for each butterfly species.

Gray Hairstreak

Strymon melinus

Wingspan: 1" – 1 1/2"

Host plants: Hops, Legumes, Mallows, Cotton

Broods per year: 1 - 2

Overwinter as: Pupae

Hairstreaks are small, fast-flying butterflies that have dark streak-like markings on the undersides of their wings. Most also have hair-like projections on their tails. They tend to be mostly gray or brown in color and most have one or more orange or red spots near the bottom edge of their hindwing.

Many Hairstreaks perch head down with the hair-like tail projections (which resemble antennae) and the orange or red spots (which mimic eyes) pointed up in the air. Likely this is a defense mechanism. If a bird attacks them, it will aim for what looks like the head, only to take a bite from the butterfly's tail. With just a bite taken from the tail, the butterfly will still be able to escape.

There are numerous Hairstreaks native to the U.S. Just to name a few, there is the Gray Hairstreak featured on this page (which is also known as the Cotton Borer), the Banded Hairstreak, the Hickory Hairstreak, the Red-Banded Hairstreak, the Coral Hairstreak, and the White M Hairstreak. Some hairstreaks prefer to reside near forests while others are regular visitors to urban gardens. Most Hairstreaks find Milkweed irresistible when it is blooming.

Wherever you live in the U.S., there are likely several Hairstreaks that are indigenous to your vicinity. To distinguish one from another, though, you would likely need a field guide.

In April and May, you can often lure Commas, Question Marks, Red Admirals, Mourning Cloaks, and other fruit-seeking butterfies to a concoction made by combining 1/2 overripe banana, 1 teaspoon sugar, 1/4 teaspoon yeast, and 1/4 cup stale beer. Bad as it smells, butterflies love this stuff!

Each species of Swallowtail caterpillar is equipped with a retractable forked scent gland called an **osmeterium**. *Osmeteriums range in color from yellow to red. When the caterpillar senses danger, it exposes its osmeterium to emit a foul odor. The nasty smell quickly chases most potential predators away, deciding they would not want to swallow anything that smells that bad.*

This is a Spicebush Swallowtail caterpillar (like the one shown on page 53) with its osmeterium exposed.

Pearl Crescent

Phyciodes tharos

Wingspan: 1 1/4" – 1 3/4"

Host plants: Asters

Broods per year: 1 - 3

Overwinter as: Larvae

The white arrows point to the pearl-colored crescent which gives this butterfly its name.

The Pearl Crescent is a small butterfly that is dull brown-orange and black. It has a wide black band along the margin of its forwing and hindwing. Along the hindwing border are black spots. Irregular black splotches sprinkle the rest of the forewing and hindwing. On the underside of its hindwing, you will see a pearl-colored crescent shape which is outlined in black. Aside from that, its undersides are mostly cream and orange-brown.

The Pearl Crescent is resident to most of the U.S. Excluded from its range are California, Oregon, and Nevada. In its natural habitat, this butterfly is most abundant in open, weedy areas, in pastures and meadows, and along roadsides. They are common from May through September, and most abundant July through late August.

Pearl Crescents fly low to the ground and often glide while in flight. They are regular visitors to the garden and are particularly fond of Oxeye (*Heliopsis helianthoides*) and Gloriosa Daisy (*Rudbeckia hirta*), two flower species not regularly visited by other butterflies. Males engage in puddling.

Female Pearl Crescents lay their eggs in mass on Aster. When the caterpillars hatch, they feed communally within a web that they create themselves.

For many butterfly species, the only way to distinguish a male from a female is by examining the abdomens. If it has claspers (as shown on page 10), it is a male. If not, it's a female.

On some of the larger butterflies, it is relatively easy to distinguish a male from a female, even in the field. Smaller butterflies have to be netted, and sometimes examined with a magnifying glass, to decipher the sex.

If your interest in butterflies strengthens and you want to purchase a quality insect net, I recommend BioQuip Products as a reputable source for professional, quality nets. Their website address is www.BioQuip.com.

Eastern Tailed Blue

Everes comyntas

Wingspan: 3/4" – 1"

Host plants: Clover, Alfalfa, False Indigo, Beans, Peas

Broods per year: 3

Overwinter as: Larvae

The irridescent blue color of this Eastern Tailed Blue identifies it as a male.

The Eastern Tailed Blue is one of our smallest butterflies. They generally flutter slowly, almost lazily, and often stay close to the ground. The male Eastern Tailed Blue is iridescent blue while the female is brownish-gray with blue at the base of her hindwing. On the underside, the butterfly is predominately gray with a splotch of orange on the outer margin of its hindwing.

The range of the Eastern Tailed Blue includes the eastern half of the U.S., west to North Dakota, and south to Florida and Texas. They are generally found in open grassy areas. Eastern Tailed Blues are commonly seen May through October, but are most abundant July through September. They can be encouraged to visit the butterfly garden by providing Common Milkweed, Coreopsis, low-growing Zinnia, and Aster. The males often participate in puddling.

The female lays her eggs on the flower buds of host plants, rather than on the leaves as most other butterflies do. When the caterpillars hatch, they feed strictly on the buds, flowers, and seeds.

The Western Tailed Blue looks very similar to the Eastern Tailed Blue. It is indigenous to the western half of the country.

Eastern Tailed Blues are among the butterflies that puddle. Here a group of five males are puddling.

In the beginning of the book, I thanked the people who so graciously allowed me to use their photographs in my book. Again, I would like to express gratitude to these contributors: Edith Smith, Jim Nero, Tom Pawlesh, Paul Chestefield, Michael Keniston, and Tatia Veltkamp. Without them, Part V might have excluded several of the butterfly species that I had previously planned to feature. In the back of the book, you will find more information about each of these contributors.

The Butterflies You Might See In Your Garden 75

Butterfly gardening often leads to an interest in butterfly photography. But don't assume you have to spend two thousand dollars on a camera to get great photos. Andy, my husband, uses a Cannon Power Shot while I use my Nikon Coolpix. Both take beautiful close-ups and each sells for less than $200. Then, to take our captured images from great to absolutely stunning, I edit them in Photoshop Elements.

Gulf Fritiallaries are year-around residents in south Florida and south Texas. In summer, they migrate north to populate the southeastern portion of the U.S. Then they might be spotted as far north as Kansas, Missouri, Kentucky, West Virginia, and Virginia. Occasionally, they are seen here in central Pennsylvania. Gulf Fritillaries lay their eggs on Passionvine (aka Passion Flower).
Top: A Gulf Fritillary laying an egg. Below: An arrow points to the egg just laid.

Part VI

Sharing The Sources

Part VI: Sharing The Sources

Over the years, I purchased and read a lot of wonderful books pertaining to butterflies and/or butterfly gardening. I also found some great websites on the Internet. So that you might enjoy some of the books and websites I was fortunate enough to find, I will list many of my favorites here.

Books:

The Butterfly Book: An Easy Guide to Butterfly Gardening, Identification, and Behavior, by Donald and Lillian Stokes, 1991, ISBN: 978-0316817806.
This was the first book I purchased on butterflies and it is still my favorite. It presents groups of butterflies according to the family they belong to. The concept of butterfly families was barely touched in my book but it is both interesting and important. The book includes distribution maps for the butterflies highlighted in it.

The Family Butterfly Book: Projects, Activities, and a Field Guide to 40 Favorite North American Species, by Rick Mikula, 2000, ISBN: 978-1580172929.
In his book, Rick Mikula covers butterfly gardening, butterfly rearing, and much more. As the title implies, the book is packed with fun-filled projects and activities for the whole family.

Butterfly Gardening: Creating Summer Magic in Your Garden, 1998, ISBN: 978-0871566157.
Created by The Xerces Society, in association with The Smithsonian Institution. This book's chapters were written by various authors including Miriam Rothschild, Jo Brewer, Robert Michael Pyle.

The Butterfly Garden: Creating Beautiful Gardens to Attract Butterflies, by Jerry Sedenko, 1991, ISBN: 0-394-58982-3.
Jerry Sedenko explains the portrayal of butterflies throughout history, illustrates numerous plants and butterflies that might be seen in butterfly gardens, offers suggestions on butterfly garden planning, and more.

Field Guides:

Butterflies Through Binoculars: A Field Guide to Butterflies in the Boston-New-York-Washington Region, by Jeffrey Glassberg, 1993, ISBN: 0-19-507983-3.
Jeffrey Glassberg explains how to find and identify the nearly 160 species of butterflies that inhabit the Northeast. For each butterfly species illustrated in the book, its range, flight periods, and host plants are listed. The field guide includes approximately 300 beautiful, full-color photographs.

A Field Guide to Eastern Butterflies, by Paul A. Opler, 1992, ISBN: 0-395-63279-X.
Another wonderful field guide. This book describes every butterfly species found east of the Great Plains, from Greenland to Mexico, 524 species in all. It also includes range maps which show where each species is likely to be found.

National Audubon Society Field Guide to North American Butterflies, by Robert Michael Pyle, 1997 (twelfth printing), ISBN: 0-394-51914-0.
This is a beautiful field guide. The book covers 600 species in detail with notes provided on 70 others. Included in the guide are 1,014 full-color identification photographs showing living butterflies, larvae, and chrysalises in their natural habitats.

Peterson First Guide to Caterpillars of North America, by Amy Bartlett Wright, 1993, ISBN: 0-395-56499-9.
This was the first field guide to caterpillars that I purchased and I still cherish this little book. It is small enough that it can be tucked into a small camera bag or purse and taken anywhere. The guide features 120 of the most common caterpillars, butterflies and moths, in North America. Also included in the book is information on how to raise caterpillars, where to find them, and what to feed them.

Caterpillars of Eastern North America: A Guide to Identification and Natural History, by David L. Wagner, ISBN: 0-691-12144-3.
This beautiful guide illustrates the caterpillars of nearly 700 butterflies and moths found east of the Mississippi. It includes 1,200 color photos and information on the distribution, seasonal activity, foodplants, and life cycle of the caterpillars illustrated.

Websites:

www.ButterfliesAndMoths.org
On this website you will find information and range maps for most of the butterflies and moths of North America. Their image gallery is chock-full of photos, too. What an ambitious effort to collect, store, and share species information and occurrence data on butterflies and moths.

www.GardensWithWings.com
From the home page of this beautiful website, you can enter your zip code, click on 'Go', and immediately be presented with pictures of the butterflies you might be able to attract to your garden. Then, you can check the boxes of the butterflies you hope to attract, click on 'View Butterflies and Plants', and be presented with a list of nectar plants and host plants you should plant on your property.

www.ButterflyFunFacts.com
On this website you can learn more about butterfly life cycles and butterfly parasitoides and diseases. You will also find information on how to raise many species of butterflies.

www.ButterflyWebsite.com
The Butterfly Website is the world's oldest and largest website dedicated to butterflies and moths. Here you will find lots of articles, photos, videos, and clip art pertaining to butterflies and moths.

www.MonarchWatch.org
Monarch Watch is a cooperative network of students, teachers, volunteers, and researchers dedicated to the education, conservation, and research of the Monarch butterfly. The project is directed by Dr. O. R. "Chip" Taylor, Dept. of Entomology, University of Kansas.

www.NABA.org
The North American Butterfly Association website offers information on butterfly gardening, butterfly identification, and much more.

www.learner.org/jnorth
The home of Journey North. Among other things, Journey North tracks the migration patterns of Monarch butterflies, hummingbirds, robins, whopping cranes, gray whales, bald eagles, and more. A wonderful resource for teachers and students.

www.RaisingButterflies.org
Here you will find instruction for rearing numerous species of butterflies. You will learn that Monarchs, Painted Ladies, Red Admirals, Common Buckeyes, and more are relatively easy to rear. All you'll need is a small plastic aquarium with a screened lid.

www.xerces.org
The Xerces Society is a nonprofit organization that protects wildlife through the conservation of invertebrates and their habitat. On their website you will find information on bees, beetles, butterflies and moths, dragonflies, and more.

www.plants.usda.gov
Home of the USDA Natural Resources Conservation Service. This gigantic plant database will help you find the plants that are native to your state. You can also learn about noxious and invasive plants, wetland plants, and the endangered plants of the U.S.

www.DavesGarden.com
Dave's Garden is a huge website that offers all kinds of information on plants and gardening. Over 100 forums are available for asking questions on any gardening topic. You can utilize the 'Plant Scout' to find plants or seeds you are looking for.

www.GardenWeb.com
A great resource for gardeners. Over a hundred forums, seed and plant exchanges, and the HortiPlex Database, which contains information on over 50,000 plant cultivars.

DVD/Blu-Ray:
Metamorphosis: The Beauty and Design of Butterflies (2011)
Spectacular photography captures the metamorphosis of butterflies close-up—and you will be amazed! The film also features beautiful footage of the Monarch's annual migration from Canada to Mexico. A pro-creation release, the film runs approximately 64 minutes.

Available at www.MetamorphosisTheFilm.com, www.Amazon.com, and many other retailers.

An Invitation to Explore My Website

You might also want to visit my website, www.ButterflyBushes.com, where I offer many of the perennials that I recommend for incorporation into the butterfly garden. As I stated early in the book, my perennial nursery has been a test ground in my search for the best-of-the-best butterfly plants.

I am sorry to say that because my plants are shipped as outdoor-grown potted plants, I am only permitted to ship to 27 states. We ship to Alabama, Arkansas, Connecticut, Delaware, Georgia, Illinois, Indiana, Kentucky, Massachusetts, Maryland, Maine, Michigan, Minnesota, Missouri, North Carolina, New Hampshire, New Jersey, New York, Ohio, Pennsylvania, Rhode Island, South Carolina, Tennessee, Virginia, Vermont, West Virginia, and Wisconsin. The USDA Japanese Beetle Quarantine restricts me from shipping plants to any other state.

You might also want to check out my Facebook page.

www.Facebook.com/Rose.Franklin.Perennials

www.ButterflyBushes.com

Why the USDA Imposed the Japanese Beetle Quarantine

Japanese Beetles are destructive insects. They feed on the foliage, flowers, and fruit of over 300 plant species. They can defoliate a plant when they attack in large numbers.

Japanese Beetles are native to Japan, where they are not much of a problem because natural predators keep their numbers in check. Somehow, Japanese Beetles were introduced into the U.S. in 1916, first being spotted in Riverton, N.J. Since then, they have spread across the eastern U.S. and are now numerous in most of the states that lie east of the Mississippi River.

Japanese Beetles lay their eggs in soil. The eggs hatch in eight to fourteen days. The larvae, which are grubs, feed mostly on grass roots and can severely damage lawns, golf courses, and pasture fields. In October, the grubs dig deeper into the soil to over-winter. The next spring, around mid-April, they come out of hibernation, begin to feed again, grow to a mature size of about 1" long, and then pupate. In June, adult beetles begin to emerge from the pupae and rampantly feed on foliage, flowers, and fruit.

Because they can be quite destructive, the USDA imposed the Japanese Beetle Quarantine. The quarantine restricts the movement of soil that could potentially be infected with Japanese Beetle eggs and/or larvae into areas not yet heavily infected with this insect. Since many of my plants are grown outdoors during the summer, Japanese Beetles eggs and/or larvae could potentially be in the soil. Hence, my plants cannot be shipped to those states which are not yet heavily infected with Japanese Beetles.

How To Contact The Author

I am sorry to say that my nursery is not open for retail sales. Orders are accepted via the website only.

I wish I could invite people to come see our gardens but unfortunately, summers are extremely busy here. Working fourteen hour days from April through September, I simply do not have the time for visitors.

When I am able to retire, I would like to invite butterfly enthusiasts for leisurely tours of our gardens, but until I retire and have spare time, I simply cannot do that.

We do occasionally offer seminars on butterfly gardening, at which time we allow attendees to explore our gardens. But because of time restraints, we generally do not offer more than one or two seminars a year. Our Gardening for Butterflies seminars are always advertised on the website and on our Facebook page.

If you have questions or comments pertaining to this book, or pertaining to butterfly gardening in general, please email me at RoseFranklin@aol.com. If you do not have access to a computer, you may write to me at Rose Franklin, 107 Butterfly Lane, Spring Mills, PA 16875.

I hope I have inspired you to create a butterfly garden; and if I have, I hope you enjoy your garden as much as I enjoy mine.

Rose M. Franklin

About The People Who Contributed Photographs......

Edith Smith and her husband, Stephen, operate Shady Oak Butterfly Farm. Located in Brooker, FL, they offer several species of butterflies for release at weddings and other special events. Their website address is www.ButterfliesEtc.com.

Jim Nero resides in Louisville, OH, and oversees the butterfly house at Beech Creek Botanical Garden and Nature Preserve in Alliance, OH. The website address for the Botanical Garden and Nature Preserve is www.bcbgarden.org.

Tom Pawlesh lives in Pittsburgh, PA, where he is an airline pilot and wildlife photographer. He has flown a variety of aircraft, from corporate jets to airliners, and currently flies for US Airways. Some of his beautiful photos can be seen at www.TomPawlesh.smugmug.com.

Michael Keniston hails from the Tampa Bay area in Florida. He is a butterfly breeder, artist, and macro-photographer. His other interests include carpentry, painting, sculpture, scuba diving, gardening, theater, and travel. His website can be found at www.ACloserEyeView.com.

Paul Chesterfield lives in Gosport, England. He is a wonderful photographer and published **Images from Nature** in 2008. This large, coffee-table style book includes over 200 of the author's favorite photographs that show the wonder of nature close-up. Paul's website is at www.PaulCPhotography.com.

Tatia Veltcamp operates the Wings of Enchantment Butterfly Farm in Albuquerque, NM. She offers educational presentations in local schools and ships live, hand-reared butterflies to customers wanting to release them at special events. Her website address is www.WingsOfEnchantment.com.

Glossary of Butterfly Terminology

Abdomen
The last of three sections of a butterfly's body. The abdomen is composed of ten segments and contains the reproductive organs. Digestive and excretory functions also occur here.

Antenna (singular)
Antennae (plural)
Located on the butterfly's head, these appendages are equipped with chemical receptors that serve the function of smelling. They also assist the butterfly in balance.

Caterpillar
Larva. The second stage in the life cycle of a butterfly.

Chrysalis (singular)
Chrysalises, Chrysalides (plural)
Pupa. The shell that encases a caterpillar to protect it as it transforms into butterfly.

Cremaster
The hook-like appendage at the end of a caterpillar's abdomen which is utilized to attach the caterpillar to its silk-like pad for pupation.

Eclose
Eclosure. Eclosion. The moment when a butterfly emerges from its chrysalis (pupa).

Egg
The first stage in the life cycle of a butterfly.

Exoskeleton
The hard covering that provides support and protection for an insect's body.

Frass
The waste product (poop) excreted by a caterpillar (larva).

Hemolymph
The blood-like substance of insects which is usually yellowish in color.

Instar
The period between caterpillar molts. There are generally five instars during the larval stage.

Larva (singular)
Larvae (plural)
Caterpillar. The second stage in the life cycle of a butterfly.

Lepidoptera
The order of insects which includes butterflies and moths.

Molting
The shedding of skin. Most butterfly larvae molt five times during the larval stage of development.

Osmeterium
A fleshy, Y-shaped, retractable gland found on the head of Swallowtail larvae. When exposed, the gland emits an odor so foul it wards off most predators.

Oviposit
The laying of eggs.

Pheromone
A scent emitted by the males of some species of butterflies making him attractive to females.

Proboscis
The straw-like apparatus located on a butterfly's head which is used for feeding (the intake of liquids). When not in use, it is coiled up under the butterfly's head.

Prolegs
The five pair of leg-like appendages on the abdomen of a caterpillar's body.

Pupa (singular)
Pupae (plural)
Chrysalis. The third stage in the life cycle of a butterfly. The stage in which a caterpillar transforms into a butterfly.

Pupate
The shedding of skin which occurs as a caterpillar (larva) becomes a pupa (chrysalis).

Spinneret
The organ located on the head of a caterpillar which is used for creating silk-like threads.

Spiracles
The small openings on the skin of insects through which they breathe.

Tentacles
Filaments. Fleshy antennae-like extensions at the front or rear of caterpillars which are used as sense organs.

Thorax
The middle portion of a butterfly's body. Composed of three segments, the butterfly's two pair of wings and three pair of legs are attached to the thorax.

A last minute update.......

On page 25, I stated that I planted a few Pawpaw trees on our property in 2011 with the hope of attracting Zebra Swallowtails for egg-laying. Well guess what. Andy, my husband, found a large Zebra Swallowtail caterpillar on one of our Pawpaw trees on June 30, 2012. The caterpillar pupated the next day and a beautiful butterfly emerged from the chrysalis on July 16.

During the next week, we saw four Zebra Swallowtails in our yard and on July 23, we watched a female deposit eggs on a tray of Pawpaw seedlings that was sitting on one of our nursery benches. We brought the seedlings into the greenhouse so that the eggs would be protected from predators.

Andy and I counted over two dozen Zebra Swallowtail eggs on the Pawpaw seedlings and as of July 31, the day the pages of my book are being sent off to the publisher for printing, most of the eggs have hatched. We are pretty excited!

Pictured below are two photos of the first Zebra Swallowtails to have been reared on one of the Pawpaws that were planted in our yard last summer.

Made in the USA
Middletown, DE
10 June 2015